Reading Drills

FOR SPEED AND COMPREHENSION

EDWARD B. FRY, Ph.D.
Professor Emeritus
Rutgers University

JAMESTOWN PUBLISHERS

Reading Drills
FOR SPEED AND COMPREHENSION

Introductory Level

Catalog No. 841
© 1989 by Edward B. Fry

Cover and Text Design by Deborah Christie
Cover photograph by Warren Jagger

Printed in the United States of America

4 5 6 GG 98 97 96

ISBN: 0-89061-531-4

Foreword

This Introductory Level of *Reading Drills for Speed and Comprehension* is new; we have split our Middle Level text (now designated Intermediate Level) and part of it has reemerged here in a drill book for younger readers. Many of the stories appearing at this level are from well-known children's books.

With this change, *Reading Drills* now comprises three drill books:

Introductory Level for Grades 4–6
Intermediate Level for Grades 6–8
Advanced Level for Grades 7–10

Another major change in *Reading Drills* is the replacement of cloze drills with maze drills. The former cloze tests were completion tasks, requiring the reader to supply the missing word; maze tests provide a choice of answers for each blank. The maze activity matches that needed for success on the DRP (Degrees of Reading Power) and other current reading tests. With maze drills there is more emphasis on comprehension of content and less emphasis on knowledge of syntax (grammar). In addition cloze and maze items use the exact words and sentences of the passage and do not require the additional reading of a question.

Both the Introductory and Intermediate Level drill books are patterned after my original (and very successful) *Reading Drills for Speed and Comprehension* that is used in many secondary school and college reading improvement courses.

This text is introducing a new element into the upper elementary reading curriculum, that of reading for speed or, put more academically, reading rate improvement. Not that reading rate hasn't been discussed, researched, and, in a few instances, taught at the elementary level, but rather it just isn't frequently taught. Two of my former graduate students, Dr. James Swalm and Dr. Marion Kimberly, have both amply demonstrated that reading improvement training, such as is recommended in this book, works quite well with intermediate-aged, and even elementary, children. Their research tended to show that doubling the reading rate from 150 to 300 words per minute was not uncommon for these children. However, individual students vary, and poor readers should be given plenty of reading practice and comprehension training before encouraging reading rate improvement.

Generally speaking, any age individual, second grade through adult, can improve reading rate with training. Caution should be exercised, however, in believing some newspaper claims of extremely rapid rate gains in short periods of time—the courses cited usually teach just a skimming technique.

An important factor in rate training is that rate improvement is best accomplished on material that is a little on the easy side for the individual student. Hence, if you have a student who is working at or below the readability levels in this book, you might best use the drills for just comprehension training. Readability for each story is shown in the table of contents with each story title.

These drills will work fine for just reading comprehension training and vocabulary improvement. If those are your only goals, omit the timing and encouragement of speed improvement.

However, you will find that average and, particularly, above-average students greatly enjoy reading speed improvement.

Another teaching feature of this book is our desire to encourage students to do as much sustained reading as possible. To that end we have encouraged the student to continue the reading of the story started in each drill by obtaining the whole book from a school or public library. We hope that you will follow through with this suggestion.

And now, please read the section addressed to the teacher using this book. The information contained there will help you to teach this program much more effectively and give you some background on the reading skills and techniques which are included.

Finally, I hope that both you and the students like this book; if not, tell me.

I would like to acknowledge the valuable assistance of Robert Hayes and Cathy Lyttle in preparing this edition.

Edward Fry

Acknowledgments

Acknowledgment is gratefully made to the following authors, agents, and publishers for permission to reprint excerpts from these works.

"Tuck Everlasting" from *Tuck Everlasting* by Natalie Babbitt. Copyright © 1975 by Natalie Babbitt. Reprinted by permission of Farrar, Straus & Giroux, Inc.

"The Adventures of the Black Cowboys" from *The Adventures of the Black Cowboys* by Philip Durham and Everett L. Jones. Copyright © 1965, 1966 by Philip C. Durham and Everett L. Jones. Reprinted by permission of Dodd, Mead & Company, Inc.

"A Taste of Blackberries" from *A Taste of Blackberries* by Doris Buchanan Smith. Reprinted by permission of Harper & Row, Publishers, Inc.

"How to Lasso a Shark" by William B. McMorris. Reprinted by permission of *Boy's Life* magazine.

"J. T." from *J. T.* by Jane Wagner. Reprinted by permission of Van Nostrand Reinhold.

"Mystery Monsters of Loch Ness" from *Mystery Monsters of Loch Ness* by Patricia Lauber. Copyright © 1978 by Patricia Lauber. Reprinted by permission of the Garrard Publishing Company, Champaign, Illinois.

"The Great Brain at the Academy" from *The Great Brain at the Academy* by John D. Fitzgerald. Copyright © 1972 by John D. Fitzgerald. Used by permission of the publisher, The Dial Press.

"Wilt Chamberlain" from *Wilt Chamberlain* by Kenneth Rudeen. Copyright © 1970 by Kenneth Rudeen. Reprinted by permission of Thomas Y. Crowell, Publishers.

"From the Mixed-Up Files of Mrs. Basil E. Frankweiler" from *From the Mixed-Up Files of Mrs. Basil E. Frankweiler* by E. L. Konigsburg. Copyright © 1967 by E. L. Konigsburg. Reprinted by permission of Atheneum Publishers, an imprint of Macmillan Publishing Company.

"The World of Robots" from *The World of Robots* by Jonathan Rutland. Copyright © 1978 by Grisewood & Dempsey Ltd. Reprinted by permission.

"Mom, You're Fired!" from *Mom, You're Fired!* by Nancy K. Robinson. Copyright © 1981 by Nancy K. Robinson. Reprinted by permission of Scholastic, Inc.

"We Live in Mexico" from *We Live in Mexico* by Carlos Somonte. Copyright by Carlos Somonte. Reprinted by permission of the publisher, Franklin Watts, Inc.

"A Bear Called Paddington" from *A Bear Called Paddington* by Michael Bond. Copyright © 1958 by Michael Bond. Reprinted by permission of Houghton Mifflin Company and Curtis Brown, Ltd.

"Charlie and the Chocolate Factory" from *Charlie and the Chocolate Factory* by Roald Dahl. Copyright © 1964 by Roald Dahl. Reprinted by permission of Alfred A. Knopf, Inc.

"They Study the Ocean" from *Jobs That Save Our Environment* by Melvin Berger. Copyright © 1973 by Melvin Berger. Reprinted by permission of Lothrop, Lee and Shepard Books (a division of William Morrow and Company, Inc.)

"Hotel for Dogs" from *Hotel for Dogs* by Lois Duncan. Copyright © 1971 by Lois Duncan Arquette. Reprinted by permission of Harold Ober Associates, Inc.

"Birth of an Island" from *Birth of an Island* by Millicent E. Selsam. Text copyright © 1959 by Millicent E. Selsam. Reprinted by permission of Harper & Row, Publishers, Inc.

Contents

Set 4

Set 5

Set 6

How to Use This Book

1. **Have the students time themselves while reading a passage.**
   On an individual basis this can best be done using a stopwatch, but on a group basis the teacher can write the elapsed time every 10 seconds on the chalkboard using any watch with a second hand as a timer. Students should *write down the time* it took to read the passage as soon as they finish reading it.

2. **Have the students do the drills without looking back at the passage.** It is best to do all the drills now but if time is not available, just the Comprehension Drill can be done. The drills are not timed.

3. **Have the students correct (score) the drills using the table and answer keys at the back of the book.**

4. **The students should then enter their scores on the progress graphs at the back of the book.**

5. **Interpretation of progress is important.**
   a. First look at the balance between speed and comprehension. See the next section, *Background for the Instructor*, for more information on proper balance.
   b. When interpreting comprehension scores, keep in mind that the first 4 questions are factual and the second 4 are inferential. Also see comprehension suggestions in *Background for the Instructor*.
   c. Maze drills essentially measure passage comprehension, but, unlike multiple choice comprehension questions, maze items are presented in context. This means that the reader is less dependent on retention of information gained under timed reading conditions.
   d. In part, the vocabulary drills measure general word knowledge, but in addition they give the student an opportunity to develop ability in using context (the surrounding words) as an aid to word recognition and vocabulary development.

6. **Encouragement is important.**
   Students need the discipline of regular assignments and class drill time. They also need encouragement from the teacher on a regular and sustained basis. A further form of encouragement is seeing progress on the graphs. Most do-it-yourself or home-improvement reading courses fail because of lack of teacher discipline, stimulation, and encouragement.

7. **Assignments.** There are thirty drills in the book, grouped into six sets. This may be considered six weeks of work at the rate of one drill per day. Or the teacher may assign the drills at any

feasible rate such as two or three drills per week. If drills are assigned for homework, at least one drill per week should be done in class. If speed improvement is one of the objectives, one drill per week is probably spreading it out too thin.

8. Comprehension only. This drill book may be used for just reading comprehension without emphasis on speed. In this instance don't time the passages and have the student concentrate on getting the highest possible scores on the Comprehension, Maze, and Vocabulary drills.

9. Answer keys. The answer keys at the end of the book can be removed if the teacher deems it appropriate. The teacher can score the drills or the students can trade papers and score the drills of each other while the teacher reads the answers aloud. However, in many classes self-scoring works well with students using the answer keys at the back of the book. Occasionally a student will disagree with the answer given in the key. Spirited class discussions can result when students must "prove" that their answer is correct and find the supporting passage.

Background for the Instructor

Reading Drills, Introductory Level is designed as a drill book to help students at elementary levels improve their reading speed and comprehension.

This drill book emphasizes timed reading passages followed by comprehension questions, a maze passage, and a vocabulary in context drill. Timed reading is the best known method of improving reading speed. The comprehension drills are a way of continually pointing out to students that there is no point in reading at any speed if there is no understanding.

Readability of the Passages

The thirty reading passages have all been graded for readability and arranged in the following order: The first passage in every set of five passages is of medium difficulty, readability level 5; the other passages range in difficulty from levels 3 to 7. Thus the student has the advantage of reading passages of varying difficulty. However, for measuring growth in reading rate, it is preferable to use passages of equal difficulty. You will note that the reading rate progress graph on page 213 has columns for each passage in the book. We recommend, however, that the student graph only the first passage in a set, or an average of the five passages in a set. The reason that we do not ask the student to plot every passage on the graph is that improvement tends to show a lot of variability, and it is easier to see progress

when either the averages or the first passages are used. Another reason is that in some courses certain passages are used in class, and others assigned as homework. The reading rates for passages done as homework show variability because of many factors, ranging from inaccurate timing to disruptive environmental conditions. Reading rate tends to jump around quite a bit anyway due to fatigue, fluctuations in motivation, previous knowledge of the subject, and many other factors. Hence, we are suggesting you control at least a few of these causes for fluctuation by consistently having the student graph the first passage or a unit average.

Assigning Drills

There is no fixed time for completing a unit, but sets of five suggest a week's work, along with whatever other projects the instructor assigns. A maximum of ten weeks has often been found to be a satisfactory time period to work on reading rate improvement—short enough to hold interest and long enough to gain some practice experience and to start establishing new habits.

Reading Speed Improvement

Training in reading rate improvement can benefit almost everyone. In the United States some of the most enthusiastic students in reading improvement courses are university graduates who realize how important even a slight improvement in reading skill can be. I am happy to report that reading rate training is becoming a regular part of many university and secondary school curricula.

Improvement of reading speed, at any level, is for the average or superior student. Students having difficulty in reading should concentrate on comprehension before working to improve speed. This drillbook may be used primarily for comprehension improvement, if that is what the teacher wishes to emphasize. (See below.) In that case, timing can be omitted.

As a rule, the passages in a reading speed improvement book should be relatively easy for the student. The student should not have difficulty with the vocabulary or the subject matter. Hence, most of the passages in this book should be fairly easy for elementary students. Don't worry about their being too easy; the student should see how quickly and efficiently he or she can read them. One mark of good readers is the ability to speed up and read rapidly easy material, while maintaining good comprehension. Conversely, one mark of poor readers is that they read everything at the same speed, usually slow.

Comprehension

There is nothing more important than comprehension in reading: the main purpose in reading is to understand the author's thoughts.

The multiple choice questions that follow each of the selections in this drill book are divided into two types of questions. The first four questions are matters of fact and the second four questions require the ability to put several different ideas together to form a new idea, or the ability to discover what is meant although not specifically stated. These latter questions might be called subjective because they require some thinking on the part of the reader.

Very few students can read these passages once and get all of the multiple choice questions correct. Usually a score of 70 or 80 percent correct is normal. If the student is getting 90 or 100 percent correct, he or she is probably reading too slowly for the purposes of the exercises in this course and should speed up. A comprehension score below 70 percent indicates a need for improvement.

You should be aware that there will be fluctuations in comprehension, from the same causes as fluctuations in reading rate. There is a further cause for fluctuations in comprehension. The comprehension questions and maze passages are really drills, not reliable test instruments. Hence, you should look upon them as indications of comprehension achievement. Unit averaging, of course, produces more stable scores, but even working passage-by-passage, the student and instructor will see trends in comprehension ability. Don't expect the scores to be terribly accurate; after all, their chief purpose is to teach the student the importance of comprehending while reading at an improving rate.

All of the drills in this book are designed to be corrected by the student immediately after completing them. An answer key is provided on pages 201–206. Perhaps the most obvious benefit of this is that it saves the teacher work. However, the more valid reason is that it is a better learning situation for the student. Psychologists have consistently found that the more immediate the knowledge of results (right or wrong), the better the learning.

One method of improving comprehension is for the student to go back and study all of the multiple choice questions failed. First, the question must be read again very carefully. It is surprising how many students get the wrong answer simply because they have not carefully read the question. After doing this, the student should look back in the story to find the place where the question is answered. If the question is from the first half of the drill, that is, an objective or factual question, the answer should be fairly easy to find. On the other hand, an incorrect answer to a question in the second part of the drill requires more thought or inference. The portions of the story that deal with that question may have to be reread. The student should think about those portions to see how the correct answer is arrived at. The important work here is for the student to see what a correct answer looks like when it is embedded in the text. Teacher guidance or class discussion is often important in this regard in teaching comprehension.

Sometimes the student will disagree with the author's answer to a question. This is natural, particularly in questions five through eight—the subjective questions. It is quite possible for there to be legitimate differences of opinion as to a correct answer. These questions are for purposes of drill only. If the questions succeed in focusing the student's attention on the importance of comprehension, then they have accomplished their purpose.

Speed versus Comprehension

It is not unusual for students' comprehension scores to decline as they make rapid increases in speed during the early weeks of a reading improvement course. If this happens, the student should attempt to level off his or her speed—*but not lower it*—and concentrate more on comprehension. Usually, if the student maintains the higher speed and concentrates on comprehension, scores will gradually increase (within a week or two) back up to normal levels of 70 to 80 percent. The *wrong* thing to do is to decrease speed. Decreasing speed will almost immediately bring up comprehension scores, but the student may be in the awkward position of being right back where he or she started. The illustration on the next page illustrates this problem of increased speed with decreasing comprehension.

Students should keep their own speed and comprehension graphs in the back of the drill book. Achieving a proper balance between speed and comprehension is one of the most important things to learn in this course. An inefficient reader typically reads everything at one speed, usually slow. Another type of poor reader is one who reads rapidly without satisfactory comprehension.

Hence, the important thing is to achieve a balance between speed and comprehension. The training provided by this drill book enables students to increase speed while maintaining normal levels of comprehension.

Maze Drills

Higher levels of this book contained two cloze drills. Cloze drills are passages taken from the reading selection with words omitted at regular intervals. The student's task was to replace those words from recall.

This edition of *Reading Drills, Introductory Level* contains a modification of the standard cloze drill called a "maze drill." This drill has passages with words omitted, but it differs from the standard cloze technique in that the student is given five words from which to choose an answer.

Maze drills cut down on arguments over the right answer. With free recall (cloze), synonyms or grammatically correct words were often appropriate answers, but the author's exact word was the only acceptable answer.

Another reason for using the maze drill in this edition is that some current reading tests such as the DRP (Degrees of Reading Power) are now using maze items as a measure of reading achievement. The maze drills in *Reading Drills, Introductory Level* will familiarize the student with the format of that test item.

Vocabulary in Context

Accompanying each selection is a vocabulary in context exercise. These exercises consist of eight words from the selection, reprinted in context. Following each word, three meanings are given. The student's task is to select the

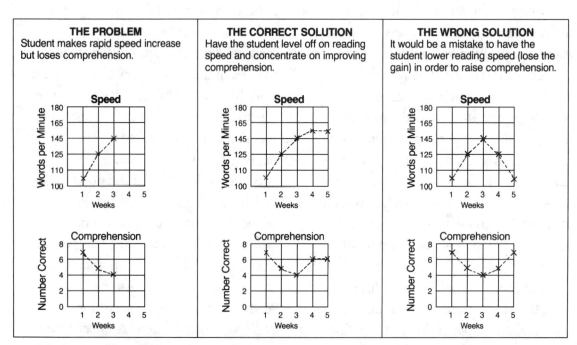

THE PROBLEM
Student makes rapid speed increase but loses comprehension.

THE CORRECT SOLUTION
Have the student level off on reading speed and concentrate on improving comprehension.

THE WRONG SOLUTION
It would be a mistake to have the student lower reading speed (lose the gain) in order to raise comprehension.

NOTE: Using the wrong approach, the student displays exactly the same speed and comprehension at the fifth week as at the first week. Hence, no improvement has taken place.

best meaning for the word as used in the selection.

The precise meaning of a word depends largely on how it is used. As you know, dictionaries often list several meanings for a single word. Only by understanding the context in which a word appears is the reader able to associate the word with an appropriate meaning.

In the vocabulary exercises each word appears in the context of the sentence or expression used in the selection. This helps the student recall how the word was originally used.

Remember to keep context in mind when completing the vocabulary exercises. More than one choice given for a word may be "dictionary correct," but only one is the best meaning for the word as used in this selection.

(We recommend that the instructor also read the next section, which is addressed to the student.)

To the Student Using This Book

The Importance of Faster Reading

You probably talk at an average rate of 150 words a minute, but, if you are a reader of average ability, you read at the rate of 250 words a minute. Thus, your reading speed, before starting the reading improvement course, is already nearly twice as fast as your speaking or listening speed. It is clear from this that reading is one of the fastest ways to put verbal knowledge into your mind. The flexibility and inexpensiveness of printing also make printed material by far the cheapest means of transmitting verbal information.

The following figure, showing the number of books read over a period of ten years, illustrates rather dramatically what an increase in reading speed can do for you. Look at the difference in the number of books read by a slow reader and those read by a good reader.

	SLOW READER (150 words per minute)	FAIR READER (250 words per minute)	GOOD READER (350 words per minute)
1 WEEK	¾ book	1¼ book	1¾ books
1 MONTH	3 books	5 books	7 books
1 YEAR	36 books	60 books	84 books
10 YEARS	360 books	600 books	840 books

The speed of 350 words a minute selected to illustrate a good reader's speed is far lower than the speeds achieved by really fast readers. However, if you are reading at a rate of 250 words a minute and can increase your speed to 350 words a minute, in the course of ten years there can be a tremendous difference in the amount of knowledge that you acquire. This illustration assumes that you will read one hour a day, six days a week, and that the books you read are of an average length of 70,000 words. Please do not assume that you must read a book for at least an hour every day. Many people do not read this much, but many would if they could learn to read better.

Faster reading, once it is mastered, makes reading more interesting, not more work.

Some Questions and Answers About Speed Reading

Here are the answers to some questions that students often ask at the beginning of a reading improvement class:

1. **How much faster will I be able to read after using this book?** Students can often double their reading speed during a class using reading matter of average difficulty. Some students will do a little better than doubling their speed. Some students make less improvement. However, even if you gain and keep a 30 or 40 percent increase, think what

this can mean when spread out through the rest of your life.

2. **Does comprehension go down when speed goes up?** Not usually. On the average, most classes end with the same comprehension that they begin with. Students whose comprehension is below normal at the beginning of a class usually manage to bring it up to normal. Other students may be reading slowly with very high comprehension. Sometimes it is better for these students to lower their comprehension a bit while trying to build speed. Your goal in this class is to become a *flexible* reader: one who can go fast when it is desirable or necessary.

3. **Can someone be too young to improve reading speed?** No. At Rutgers University in New Jersey, Dr. James Swalm was able to show meaningful improvement among fifth graders. In other experiments, Dr. Marion Kimberly improved the reading rate of pupils in grades 2, 4, 6, and 8. The average speed for each class tended to double with little or no loss in comprehension. Not every student doubled reading rate, but the class average doubled using methods discussed in the teacher's section and using drills like the ones in this book. Normally, students do improve their reading speed for each year in school, but a special class on reading speed improvement produces gains well beyond those.

4. Do all students make the same speed gains? No, there are different types of reading ability. Some students are gifted in reading, just as others may be in music or math. However, everyone can learn to read with a fairly high degree of efficiency. Further, nearly everyone can improve with training. But it is not unusual for some students to be able to read twice as fast as others. Also, during training, students may show different patterns of improvement: some make gains right away; others make no progress at first, but make sudden gains later on in the class if they continue working.

Set 1

Set 2

Set 3

Set 4

Set 5

Set 6

Answer Key

Words per Minute

Progress Graphs

Set 1

Tuck Everlasting

by Natalie Babbitt

Reading Time			Maze
Comprehension			Vocabulary

Tuck Everlasting by Natalie Babbitt is the
story of a girl who finds herself in the midst of
a frightening adventure and a great secret.
If you would like to read more of this book,
ask for it at your school or public library.

At sunset of that same long day, a stranger came strolling up the road from the village and paused at the Fosters' gate. Winnie was once again in the yard, this time intent on catching fireflies, and at first she didn't notice him. But, after a few moments of watching her, he called out, "Good evening!"

He was remarkably tall and narrow, this stranger standing there. His long chin faded off into a thin, apologetic beard, but his suit was a jaunty yellow that seemed to glow a little in the fading light. A black hat dangled from one hand, and as Winnie came toward him, he passed the other through his dry, gray hair, settling it smoothly. "Well, now," he said in a light voice. "Out for fireflies, are you?"

"Yes," said Winnie.

"A lovely thing to do on a summer evening," said the man richly. "A lovely entertainment. I used to do it myself when I was your age. But of course that was a long, long time ago." He laughed, gesturing in self-deprecation with long, thin fingers. His tall body moved continuously; a foot tapped, a shoulder twitched. And it moved in angles, rather jerkily. But at the same time he had a kind of grace, like a well-handled marionette. Indeed he seemed almost to hang suspended there in the twilight. But Winnie, though she was half charmed, was suddenly reminded of the stiff black ribbons that had hung on the door of the cottage for her grandfather's funeral. She frowned and looked at the man more closely. But his smile seemed perfectly all right, quite agreeable and friendly. "Is this your house?" asked the man, folding his arms now and leaning against the gate.

"Yes," said Winnie. "Do you want to see my father?"

"Perhaps. In a bit," said the man. "But I'd like to talk to you first. Have you and your family lived here long?"

"Oh, yes," said Winnie. "We've lived here forever."

"Forever," the man echoed thoughtfully.

It was not a question, but Winnie decided to explain anyway. "Well, not forever, of course, but as long as there've been any people here. My grandmother was born here. She says this was all trees once, just one big forest everywhere around, but it's mostly all cut down now. Except for the wood."

"I see," said the man, pulling at his beard. "So of course you know everyone, and everything that goes on."

"Well, not especially," said Winnie. "At least, *I* don't. Why?"

The man lifted his eyebrows. "Oh," he said, "I'm looking for someone. A family."

"I don't know anybody much," said Winnie, with a shrug. "But my father might. You could ask him."

"I believe I shall," said the man. "I do believe I shall."

At this moment the cottage door opened, and in the lamp glow that spilled across the grass, Winnie's grandmother appeared. "Winifred? Who are you talking to out there?"

"It's a man, Granny," she called back. "He's looking for someone."

COMPREHENSION

Read the following questions and statements. For each one, put an *x* in the box before the option that contains the most complete or accurate answer. Check your answers using the Answer Key on page 201.

1. Winnie was in her yard
   - ☐ a. exploring.
   - ☐ b. catching fireflies.
   - ☐ c. watching the sunset.

2. The stranger is
   - ☐ a. tall and bearded.
   - ☐ b. old and sad.
   - ☐ c. short and narrow.

3. As a child, the stranger also
   - ☐ a. laughed loudly.
   - ☐ b. collected fireflies.
   - ☐ c. played with a marionette.

4. The black ribbons were on Winnie's door because
   - ☐ a. it was twilight.
   - ☐ b. a stranger was near.
   - ☐ c. her grandfather had died.

5. The stranger probably stopped at Winnie's gate because
   - ☐ a. he needed directions.
   - ☐ b. he had an appointment.
   - ☐ c. she was the first person he saw as he walked.

6. The mood of this story is
   - ☐ a. funny.
   - ☐ b. mysterious.
   - ☐ c. sad.

7. At the end of the story, Winnie's grandmother called out because
   ☐ a. Winnie was talking to someone.
   ☐ b. guests were expected.
   ☐ c. she wanted to know how many fireflies were collected.

8. The man asked how long Winnie's family had lived there because he
   ☐ a. wanted to buy the land.
   ☐ b. was lost and needed directions.
   ☐ c. wanted to know about another family.

MAZE

The following passage, taken from the selection you have just read, has words omitted from it. Fill in each blank using a word from the set of five words in the column to the right of the passage. Check your answers using the Answer Key on page 201.

At sunset of that same long day, a stranger came strolling up the road from the village and paused at the Fosters' gate. Winnie was once again in the yard, this time intent on catching

_____ , and at first she
        1
didn't notice him. But, after a few moments of watching her, he called out,

"Good _____!"
              2

He was remarkably tall and narrow,

this _____ standing
              3
there. "Well, now," he said in a light voice. "Out for fireflies, are you?"

"Yes," said Winnie.

"A lovely thing to do on a summer evening," said the man richly. "I used to do it myself when I was your age." But

1. a. cold   b. him   c. bugs
   d. flies   e. fireflies

2. a. morning   b. day   c. grief
   d. night   e. evening

3. a. man   b. stranger   c. person
   d. quietly   e. being

Winnie, though she was half charmed, was suddenly reminded of the stiff black ribbons that had hung on the door of the cottage for her grandfather's

_____ . She frowned
and looked at the man more closely. But his _____ seemed perfectly all right, quite agreeable and friendly. "Is this your house?" asked the man, folding his arms now and leaning against the _____ .

"Yes," said Winnie.

"Have you and your _____ lived here long?"

"Oh, yes," said Winnie. "We've lived here _____ ."

"Forever," the man echoed thoughtfully.

4.   a. party   b. honor   c. family
          d. funeral   e. birthday

5.   a. face   b. need   c. smile
          d. greeting   e. reason

6.   a. yard   b. tree   c. gate
          d. ribbon   e. cottage

7.   a. friends   b. relatives   c. fireflies
          d. grandfather   e. family

8.   a. always   b. years   c. forever
          d. centuries   e. ages

VOCABULARY

Look at the word in boldface in each exercise that follows and read carefully the sentence with it. Put an *x* in the box before the best meaning or synonym for the word as it is used in the sentence. Check your answers using the Answer Key on page 201.

1. Winnie was once again in the yard, this time **intent** on catching fireflies.
   □ a. with great doubt
   □ b. determined
   □ c. taking a chance

2. . . . but his suit was a **jaunty** yellow that seemed to glow a little. . . .
   □ a. dirty
   □ b. spotted
   □ c. bright

3. A black hat **dangled** from one hand. . . .
   - ☐ a. hung loosely
   - ☐ b. flew
   - ☐ c. disappeared

4. "A lovely thing to do on a summer evening . . . A lovely **entertainment**."
   - ☐ a. pleasant activity
   - ☐ b. learning experience
   - ☐ c. collection

5. His tall body moved **continuously**; a foot tapped, a shoulder twitched.
   - ☐ a. like a robot
   - ☐ b. slowly
   - ☐ c. without stopping

6. At the same time he had a kind of grace, like a well-handled **marionette.**
   - ☐ a. puppet
   - ☐ b. sailor
   - ☐ c. ballet dancer

7. "I don't know anybody much," said Winnie, with a **shrug.**
   - ☐ a. a firm handshake
   - ☐ b. an intelligent smile
   - ☐ c. a lift of the shoulders

8. At this moment the cottage door opened, and in the lamp **glow** that spilled across the grass, Winnie's grandmother appeared.
   - ☐ a. flashing light
   - ☐ b. soft light
   - ☐ c. flickering light

The Adventures of the Black Cowboys

Philip Durham and Everett L. Jones

Reading Time [ ]   [ ] Maze

Comprehension [ ]   [ ] Vocabulary

The following passage was taken from *The Adventures of the Negro Cowboys* by Philip Durham and Everett L. Jones. It is the true story of Blacks—both slaves and free—who became cowboys over a hundred years ago. If you would like to read more of these adventures, ask for the book at either your school or neighborhood library.

More than a hundred years ago, before the Civil War, a crew of bronc-busting cowboys stood outside a large horse corral. With them was their boss Bradford Grimes, a cattleman who owned a large South Texas ranch near the Gulf of Mexico.

Inside the corral was a herd of wild mustangs, horses that had never been ridden. They milled around, snorting and rearing.

One of the bronc busters roped a strong stallion and held him to be saddled. Then another cowboy climbed up and tried to ride. At first the animal trotted nervously, humping a little and shying from side to side. Then it went off in high jumps, spinning and shaking and jolting its rider. Finally it put its head between its front legs, bucked high in the air, and threw the cowboy off into the dust.

Just then Mrs. Grimes, the cattleman's wife, came to the ranch house door and cried out, "Bradford! Bradford! Those Blacks are worth a thousand dollars apiece. One might get killed."

The cowboys laughed, but they knew she was telling the truth. For they were all Black slaves. Bradford Grimes was their owner.

Most of the first Black cowboys were slaves, brought by their masters from the old South. On the plantations in the South, the slaves cut cotton. On the ranches in Texas they had to learn a new trade— breaking horses and handling longhorns. Some were taught by Mexican vaqueros, some by Indians who knew the ways of horses and cattle.

Grimes was only one of hundreds of slave-owning ranchers who ran cattle in Texas. The ranchers had brought their families and slaves from Mississippi, Georgia, and other southern states. They came on horseback, on foot, and in buggies and wagons. They drove hogs, oxen, and stock.

Some ranchers settled near the Mexican border, but there they found that it was too easy for their slaves to escape. Even slaves as far north as Austin, the capital of Texas, came to think of Mexico as the promised land. As early as 1845, the year that Texas became a state, a Texas news-paper reported the escape of twenty-five Blacks. "They were mounted on some of the best horses that could be found," the story said, "and several of them were well armed." Thousands of other Black slaves escaped in the same way.

East of the Nueces River, farther from the Mexican border, most slaves found it hard to escape. So there they stayed, learning to become cowboys in bleak, rough country and learning to chase wild cattle through heavy coastal brush.

All-Black cattle crews were common throughout central and eastern Texas. There were even a few free Blacks who owned ranches before the Civil War.

Aaron Ashworth was one of them, and he owned 2,500 cattle, as well as some slaves of his own. He employed a white schoolmaster to tutor his children.

Black cowboys helped to tame and settle a wild country.

COMPREHENSION

Read the following questions and statements. For each one, put an *x* in the box before the option that contains the most complete or accurate answer. Check your answers using the Answer Key on page 201.

1. When this article begins, what is happening?
   - ☐ a. Cowboys are busting broncos.
   - ☐ b. Mrs. Grimes is calling everyone to dinner.
   - ☐ c. The slaves have all just been freed.

2. Most of the first Black slaves in Texas
   - ☐ a. had been brought there by their owners from the old South.
   - ☐ b. came on their own to look for the promised land.
   - ☐ c. came from ranches in Mexico looking for work on Texas cattle ranches.

3. How did the Black slaves on the ranches in Texas differ from those on the plantations in the old South?
   - ☐ a. They cut cotton.
   - ☐ b. They escaped from slavery.
   - ☐ c. They were mostly cowboys.

4. Many slaves escaped from Texas to
   - ☐ a. Canada.
   - ☐ b. Mexico.
   - ☐ c. South America.

5. In central and eastern Texas all-Black cattle crews were
   - ☐ a. rarely seen.
   - ☐ b. often seen.
   - ☐ c. never seen.

6. Why do you think whites and some free Blacks owned ranches and slaves in Texas?
   - ☐ a. They kept slaves because they were lonely.
   - ☐ b. They kept slaves to trade with the Indians.
   - ☐ c. Owning slaves was a cheap way to get workers.

7. The author talks about slaves before the Civil War and not after because
   ☐ a. slaves are more interesting to talk about before the Civil War.
   ☐ b. there were more slaves than ever after the Civil War.
   ☐ c. all slaves were freed after the Civil War.

8. Since the author tells you that there were hundreds of slave-owning cattle ranchers in Texas, it is possible to say that
   ☐ a. Blacks didn't help to settle Texas.
   ☐ b. Blacks helped to settle Texas.
   ☐ c. few Blacks were left in the old South.

MAZE

The following passage, taken from the selection you have just read, has words omitted from it. Fill in each blank using a word from the set of five words in the column to the right of the passage. Check your answers using the Answer Key on page 201.

Most of the first Black cowboys were slaves, brought by their masters from the old South. On the plantations in the _____ , the slaves cut cotton. On the ranches in Texas they had to learn a new trade—breaking horses and handling longhorns. Some were taught by Mexican vaqueros, some by Indians who knew the ways of _____ and cattle.

Grimes was only one of hundreds of slave-owning ranchers who ran cattle in Texas. The _____ had brought their families and slaves from Mississippi, Georgia, and other southern states. They came on horseback, on foot, and in buggies and wagons. They drove hogs, oxen, and stock.

Some ranchers settled near the

1. a. Gulf   b. West   c. state
    d. South   e. country

2. a. cowboys   b. heat   c. ranchers
    d. longhorns   e. horses

3. a. ranchers   b. slaves   c. men
    d. trains   e. wagons

_____ border, but there
they found that it was too easy for their
_____ to escape. Even
slaves as far north as Austin, the capital of
_____ , came to think
of Mexico as the promised land. As early
as 1845, the year that Texas became a
state, a Texas newspaper reported the
_____ of twenty-five
Blacks. "They were mounted on some of
the best horses that could be found," the
story said, "and several of them were well
armed." Thousands of other Black slaves
escaped in the same way.

East of the Nueces River, farther from the
Mexican border, most slaves found it hard to
escape. So there they stayed, learning to become _____ in bleak,
rough country and learning to chase wild
cattle through heavy coastal brush.

4. a. Georgian   b. Mexican   c. Texan
   d. southern   e. New Mexican

5. a. ranchers   b. cattle   c. slaves
   d. horses   e. cowboys

6. a. Texas   b. Mexico   c. South
   d. Georgia   e. Mississippi

7. a. settling   b. escape   c. purchase
   d. army   e. achievements

8. a. ranchers   b. rustlers   c. cowhands
   d. cowboys   e. crews

VOCABULARY

**Look at the word in boldface in each exercise that
follows and read carefully the sentence with it. Put an
x in the box before the best meaning or synonym for
the word as it is used in the sentence. Check your
answers using the Answer Key on page 201.**

1. Inside the corral was a herd of
   mustangs, horses that had never
   been ridden.
   □ a. wild or half-wild horses
   □ b. tame horses
   □ c. trained horses

2. Inside the corral was a herd of wild
   mustangs. . . . They **milled** around,
   snorting and rearing.
   □ a. moved in confusion
   □ b. stood quietly
   □ c. galloped and reared

3. At first the animal trotted nervously, humping a little and **shying** from side to side.
   - ☐ a. showing no fear
   - ☐ b. moving suddenly
   - ☐ c. looking around

4. On the plantations in the South, the slaves cut cotton. On the ranches in Texas they had to learn a new **trade**—breaking horses and handling longhorns.
   - ☐ a. exchange of goods
   - ☐ b. kind of work
   - ☐ c. buying and selling

5. Some were taught by Mexican **vaqueros**, some by Indians who knew the ways of horses and cattle.
   - ☐ a. bandits
   - ☐ b. settlers
   - ☐ c. cowboys

6. So there they stayed, learning to become cowboys in **bleak**, rough country and learning to chase wild cattle through heavy coastal brush.
   - ☐ a. bare and empty
   - ☐ b. cold and piercing
   - ☐ c. dark and gloomy

7. All-Black crews were **common** throughout central and eastern Texas. There were even a few free Blacks who owned ranches before the Civil War.
   - ☐ a. ordinary
   - ☐ b. cheap
   - ☐ c. expensive

8. He employed a white schoolmaster to **tutor** his children.
   - ☐ a. read to
   - ☐ b. teach
   - ☐ c. visit

A Taste of Blackberries

Doris Buchanan Smith

Reading Time [ ]   [ ] Maze

Comprehension [ ]   [ ] Vocabulary

This passage was taken from *A Taste of Blackberries* by Doris Buchanan Smith. The book tells the story of a boy who finds that a harmless prank can sometimes lead to tragedy. If you would like to read more of this book, ask for it at your school or public library.

Jamie up-and-overed the fence and started across the field. My eyes skimmed the field until they bumped into the house. I thought I saw a movement at the door.

"Jamie, come back," I screamed.

Jamie kept going and never stopped. He reached the tree, shinnied up, grabbed a couple of apples, jumped down, and started back.

The man had come out onto his porch. I fancied I saw a shotgun cradled in his arms. It was too far away for me to be sure. I ducked.

What would I do if Jamie got shot? Should I climb the fence and help him? How could I get him back over the fence? Maybe I should run for help instead.

I squeezed my eyes closed, waiting for the blast. Next thing I knew I was in the field myself, racing toward Jamie. He pushed an apple into my hand and we made tracks back to the creek. Two boys never cleared a fence so fast.

We skittered down the bank so we would be out of sight of the house.

"Did you see him?" I asked. My heart was beating paradiddles.

"Who? Him? Naw."

"He was standing on his porch watching you." Jamie raised his eyebrows with interest.

"He—" I could feel the corners of a

square knot poking inside my throat. "—had a gun."

I peeked over the bank. The day shimmered between golden sun and silver shade. Maybe there had never been a man, or a porch, or an apple tree.

But, there was the porch. There was the apple tree. And here was an apple in my hand.

"I told you he wouldn't shoot," Jamie said with false confidence.

I pushed the apple against my teeth and broke the skin. Sour-sweetness spilled into my mouth. But my stomach was spinning faster than a playground merry-go-round and wouldn't slow down to let me swallow the juice. I spit and held the fruit in front of Jamie.

"Want it?"

"Uh-uh," he grunted.

I tossed the apple and it landed with a plop in the creek. It showed white where I had taken a bite. I wondered if fish ate apples. I didn't want it to be wasted.

I glanced at Jamie. He seemed to be having trouble with his apple, too, chewing each bit a little too long. I knew he would never admit it. He would eat it or else. I looked toward the water and stared at the apple, floating like a buoy.

When he had eaten his apple to the core Jamie pitched the remains at my bobbing apple. His throw struck and the target tilted. Jamie was a good shot, with an apple core or a baseball.

We followed the creek to where it curved at the paved road. We trudged up the road, Jamie and I, not talking. I always hated to come away from the creek. One minute you were all secret and far-away feeling and the next, here you were back in the world.

COMPREHENSION

Read the following questions and statements. For each one, put an *x* in the box before the option that contains the most complete or accurate answer. Check your answers using the Answer Key on page 201.

1. Jamie stole some
   - ☐ a. apples.
   - ☐ b. fish.
   - ☐ c. blackberries.

2. The man on the porch seemed to be holding a
   - ☐ a. basket.
   - ☐ b. shotgun
   - ☐ c. cradle.

3. The narrator
   - ☐ a. made Jamie return the apples.
   - ☐ b. ate both apples.
   - ☐ c. could not eat his apple.

4. Jamie was
   - ☐ a. hoping to steal something else.
   - ☐ b. a good shot with an apple.
   - ☐ c. sick and exhausted.

5. The narrator was
   - ☐ a. confident that Jamie would return safely.
   - ☐ b. afraid that Jamie would get caught.
   - ☐ c. hoping that Jamie would get caught.

6. Jamie is
   - ☐ a. pretending to be braver than he is.
   - ☐ b. not afraid of anything.
   - ☐ c. angry with the narrator.

7. The narrator was unable to finish the apple because
   - ☐ a. it was rotten.
   - ☐ b. he had eaten too many apples.
   - ☐ c. he was upset.

8. The time that the boys spent by the creek was
   - ☐ a. dull.
   - ☐ b. special.
   - ☐ c. noisy.

**The following passage, taken from the selection you
have just read, has words omitted from it. Fill in each
blank using a word from the set of five words in the
column to the right of the passage. Check your
answers using the Answer Key on page 201.**

Jamie up-and-overed the fence and
started across the field. My eyes skimmed
the _____ until they
¹
bumped into the house. I thought I saw a
movement at the door.

"Jamie, come back," I screamed.

Jamie kept going and never

_____ . He reached
²
the tree, shinnied up, grabbed a couple of
apples, jumped down, and started back.

The man had come out onto his porch.
I fancied I saw a shotgun cradled in his
arms. It was too far away for me to be
sure. I ducked.

What would I do if Jamie got shot?
Should I climb the fence and help him?
How could I get him back over the

_____ ? Maybe I
³
should run for help instead.

I _____ my eyes
⁴
closed, waiting for the blast. Next thing I
knew I was in the field myself, racing
toward Jamie. He pushed an

_____ into my hand
⁵
and we made tracks back to the creek.
Two boys never cleared a fence so fast.

1. a. horizon   b. surface   c. area
   d. field   e. meadow

2. a. stopped   b. turned   c. slowed
   d. answered   e. fell

3. a. creek   b. fence   c. land
   d. apple tree   e. porch

4. a. shut   b. left   c. opened
   d. felt   e. squeezed

5. a. shotgun   b. tree   c. apple
   d. piece   e. fruit

We skittered down the bank so we would be out of sight of the house.

"Did you see him?" I asked. My _____ was beating paradiddles.
₆

"Who? Him? Naw."

"He was standing on his _____ watching you."
₇
Jamie raised his eyebrows with interest.

"He—" I could feel the corners of a square knot poking inside my throat. "—had a _____ ."
₈

6.   a. mind   b. breath   c. head

       d. heart   e. feet

7.   a. fence   b. porch   c. gun

       d. apple tree   e. property

8.   a. rope   b. gun   c. buoy

       d. apple   e. concern

VOCABULARY

Look at the word in boldface in each exercise that follows and read carefully the sentence with it. Put an _x_ in the box before the best meaning or synonym for the word as it is used in the sentence. Check your answers using the Answer Key on page 201.

1. My eyes **skimmed** the field until they bumped into the house.
   - ☐ a. glanced quickly over
   - ☐ b. peered closely at
   - ☐ c. squeezed tightly shut

2. He reached the tree, **shinnied** up, grabbed a couple of apples, jumped down, and started back.
   - ☐ a. walked
   - ☐ b. fell
   - ☐ c. climbed

3. I **fancied** I saw a shotgun cradled in his arms. It was too far away for me to be sure.
   - ☐ a. shouted
   - ☐ b. knew
   - ☐ c. imagined

4. We **skittered** down the bank so we would be out of sight of the house.
   - ☐ a. moved quickly
   - ☐ b. gently strolled
   - ☐ c. floated

5. The day **shimmered** between golden sun and silver shade.
   - ☐ a. burst
   - ☐ b. sparkled
   - ☐ c. stood

6. "I told you he wouldn't shoot," Jamie said with false **confidence**.
   - ☐ a. depression
   - ☐ b. act of sympathy
   - ☐ c. belief in himself

7. When he had eaten his apple to the core Jamie pitched the **remains** at my bobbing apple.
   - ☐ a. seeds
   - ☐ b. leaves
   - ☐ c. leftovers

8. We **trudged** up the road, Jamie and I, not talking.
   - ☐ a. skipped
   - ☐ b. plodded
   - ☐ c. tumbled

How to Lasso a Shark

William B. McMorris

Reading Time			Maze
Comprehension			Vocabulary

This article tells about scuba divers who round up sharks for Australia's Sea World. If you are interested in learning more about sharks or scuba diving, ask the librarian at your school or public library.

Start as if you were going to build a big butterfly net. The handle needs to be about 10 feet long. The rigid hoop is about three feet across. Instead of a net, you string a noose around the inside of the hoop with spring clips. Now, if you are like Trevor Long, associate director of Sea World near Brisbane, Australia, you are ready to hunt sharks. Trevor gets a couple of friends, puts on his scuba gear, and takes this big hoop with a rope on it down 85 feet in the sea.

The divers go to a place where a narrow channel about 30 feet deep cuts through a reef. At special times of the year, huge schools of little fish called pilchard whirl through. They are followed by hungry yellowtail kingfish that are followed by hungry sharks.

When a shark swims by, Trevor slips the hoop over the fish's head and jerks the rope tight. Another diver gets the handle and hoop out of the way and the third helps hold the rope. At this point, two men have roped a very large fish with very large teeth.

Why doesn't the shark whirl around and make a meal of a seagoing cowboy? "They almost always swim away," Trevor says.

After a battle of about 20 minutes, the shark usually gives up. The fish blows out some air bubbles and goes limp. This is a sign it is safe to bring it to the surface. If brought up too quickly, a sudden change in pressure may kill the fish.

"When they get to the top they get more life," Trevor warns. "They bite the motors, the boat, and anything else that comes in contact."

He adds quickly, "We're on the boat at this time." The crew leads the fish into a sling, winches it into a tank on board, and they run for home. Home is a 110,000-gallon tank in Sea World's Theater of the Sea.

Sea World divers put on as many as 11 shows per day about the history of diving. Audiences seated in the air-conditioned theater watch through a six-inch-thick wall of clear acrylic. It's easy to think of the fish as almost tame, just big pets in a giant aquarium. But they are not.

Sharks can fool even experts. A horrified audience watched one afternoon as a six-foot-long bronze whaler shark tore at a diver's leg for several seconds before the man could be rescued. It happened, Trevor said, after thousands of trouble-free shows. Nobody can be sure just why the attack took place.

The diver lived, the fish was replaced, but bronze whalers are watched very carefully any time a man is in the water.

Trevor credits the Boy Scouts for helping

him in his career. "Our Scoutmaster let us solve all kinds of outdoor living problems by ourselves. He also insisted we be good with knots.

I've applied both skills many times above and beneath the water."

Especially when he set up the loop of a rope that lassos sharks.

COMPREHENSION

Read the following questions and statements. For each one, put an *x* in the box before the option that contains the most complete or accurate answer. Check your answers using the Answer Key on page 201.

1. The handle of the shark lasso should be
   - ☐ a. 10 feet long.
   - ☐ b. 3 feet long.
   - ☐ c. 85 feet long.

2. Trevor Long works with sharks in
   - ☐ a. America.
   - ☐ b. Australia.
   - ☐ c. Brazil.

3. Before giving up, the shark usually battles about
   - ☐ a. 30 minutes
   - ☐ b. 20 minutes.
   - ☐ c. 16 minutes.

4. During a show at Sea World,
   - ☐ a. a bronze whaler attacked a diver.
   - ☐ b. a shark bit a motor.
   - ☐ c. Trevor Long learned some outdoor skills.

5. Scuba gear provides
   - ☐ a. protection.
   - ☐ b. oxygen.
   - ☐ c. equipment.

6. To lasso a shark in the sea, Trevor needs
   - ☐ a. one helper.
   - ☐ b. two helpers.
   - ☐ c. three helpers.

7. In this story, sharks are captured for the purpose of
   - ☐ a. scientific study.
   - ☐ b. providing food.
   - ☐ c. entertainment.

8. One can say that sharks are
   - ☐ a. peaceful.
   - ☐ b. dangerous.
   - ☐ c. easily trained.

The following passage, taken from the selection you have just read, has words omitted from it. Fill in each blank using a word from the set of five words in the column to the right of the passage. Check your answers using the Answer Key on page 201.

If you are like Trevor Long, associate director of Sea World near Brisbane, Australia, you are ready to hunt

_____ . Trevor gets a
1

couple of friends, puts on his scuba gear, and takes this big hoop with a rope on it down 85 feet in the sea.

    The _____ go to a
2

place where a narrow channel about 30 feet deep cuts through a reef. At special

times of the _____ ,
3

huge schools of little fish called pilchard whirl through. They are followed by hungry yellowtail kingfish that are followed by hungry sharks.

    When a shark swims by, Trevor slips the hoop over the fish's head and jerks the rope tight. Another diver gets the handle and hoop out of the way and the third helps hold the rope. At this point, two men have roped a very large fish with very large teeth.

    Why doesn't the shark whirl around and

make a meal of a _____
4

cowboy? "They almost always swim away," Trevor says.

    After a battle of about 20 minutes, the

1. a. lions   b. animals   c. fish
        d. sharks   e. butterflies

2. a. boats   b. crew   c. divers
        d. friends   e. fish

3. a. year   b. day   c. week
        d. month   e. season

4. a. western b. nutritious c. hungry
       d. diving e. seagoing

shark usually gives up. The fish blows out some air bubbles and goes limp. This is a sign it is _____ to bring it to the surface. If brought up too quickly, a sudden change in pressure may kill the fish.

"When they get to the top they get more life," Trevor warns. "They bite the motors, the boat, and anything else that comes in contact."

He adds quickly, "We're on the boat at this time." The _____ leads the fish into a sling, winches it into a tank on board, and they run for home. Home is a 110,000-gallon _____ in Sea World's Theater of the Sea.

Sea World divers put on as many as 11 shows per day about the history of diving. _____ seated in the air-conditioned theater watch through a six-inch-thick wall of clear acrylic.

5.   a. ready   b. okay   c. time
        d. safe   e. comfortable

6.   a. diver   b. rope   c. crew
        d. shark   e. scout

7. a. container   b. boat   c. tank
        d. jar   e. compartment

8. a. Audiences b. Divers c. Students
        d. Crews e. Families

VOCABULARY

Look at the word in boldface in each exercise that follows and read carefully the sentence with it. Put an *x* in the box before the best meaning or synonym for the word as it is used in the sentence. Check your answers using the Answer Key on page 201.

1. The **rigid** hoop is about three feet across.
   ☐ a. stiff
   ☐ b. knitted
   ☐ c. diving

2. . . . a place where a narrow **channel** about 30 feet deep cuts through a reef.
   ☐ a. wave
   ☐ b. river
   ☐ c. passage

3. Why doesn't the shark **whirl** around and make a meal of the seagoing cowboy?
   - ☐ a. twist
   - ☐ b. growl
   - ☐ c. bite

4. The fish blows out some bubbles and goes **limp**.
   - ☐ a. down
   - ☐ b. relaxed
   - ☐ c. quickly

5. "They bite the motors, the boat, and anything else that comes in **contact**."
   - ☐ a. movement
   - ☐ b. touch
   - ☐ c. noise

6. Sharks can even fool **experts**.
   - ☐ a. people who investigate situations
   - ☐ b. people who train animals
   - ☐ c. people who know all about a subject

7. A **horrified** audience watched one afternoon as a six-foot-long bronze whaler shark tore at a diver's leg for several seconds.
   - ☐ a. fascinated
   - ☐ b. shocked
   - ☐ c. surprised

8. "I've **applied** both skills many times above and beneath the water."
   - ☐ a. taught
   - ☐ b. learned
   - ☐ c. used

J. T.

Jane Wagner

Reading Time [   ]   [   ] Maze

Comprehension [   ]   [   ] Vocabulary

J. T. by Jane Wagner is the story of
an angry, troublemaking boy and his
relationship with an alley cat. If you would
like to read more of this book, ask for
it at your school or public library.

Mama Melcy leaned closer to J. T. and asked, "What you want for Christmas, child?" J. T. looked at her for a long time.

"A cat," he said. Then, gathering his determination, he continued. "I want me this cat I found. You reckon I could have him? Could I? He needs a home. He's real bad off, near dead, almost. Could I?"

A long silence followed.

His mother got up from the table and scraped the leftovers from her plate into the garbage can, then said, "I don't have me enough troubles, I got to nurse me a half-dead cat. Anyhow, only animals they allow in this place is rats."

"But Mama, he's liable to die. Please . . . couldn't I keep him? I'm afraid he'll die." J. T. looked anxiously from his mother to his grandmother.

"Well," his mother replied, "a cat's got nine lives. Losin' one won't matter much."

J. T. went into the front room and switched on the television. He had just finished supper, but somehow he felt empty inside.

Later that evening as he was getting ready for bed, Mama Melcy was unpacking her old cardboard suitcase. When she finished, she crossed over to the window. "You sure got some peculiar windows in this house, openin' out onto solid brick walls. Maybe that wall is a

machine, and if you put a quarter in and punch 'view' you'd get . . ."

"With my luck, you'd get grape soda," Rodeen replied.

Mama Melcy laughed and said, "With or without the paper cup?"

It was good having Mama Melcy around, J. T. thought. That night J. T. lay in bed with the tiny radio next to his ear. The room was dark except for the lights from across the street that visited J.T. every night.

Popping in uninvited, flexing their neon muscles . . . Bar and Grill . . . Bar/Grill/Bar/Grill . . . throbbing in and out of the room, pulsating electronic messages across J. T.'s body and over the walls. J. T. stared blankly at the lights, unable to sleep.

He wished he could send his own messages out through the night to the house where Bones was. He wondered if Bones felt as alone as he did. He closed his eyes, but sleep was nowhere inside him. He had too many feelings and worries in his head, and there was just no room for rest.

He got out of bed, dressed, and slipped quietly out the door. Maybe, he thought, the radio would make the cat feel less lonely. It had helped him, maybe it would do the same for Bones.

J. T. made his way through the night

streets. He was a little scared of his neighborhood at night. He didn't like to admit it, but he was. There were two men on the corner. They had lit a fire in a trash can and were huddled over it trying to keep warm. J. T. thought they looked lonely too.

When he reached the house, he walked as silently as he could. He didn't want to waken the cat if he was asleep.

COMPREHENSION

Read the following questions and statements. For each one, put an *x* in the box before the option that contains the most complete or accurate answer. Check your answers using the Answer Key on page 201.

1. Mama Melcy asked J. T. to
   - □ a. help her do the dishes.
   - □ b. turn down the volume on his radio.
   - □ c. tell her what he wanted for Christmas.

2. J. T. is afraid that the cat will
   - □ a. escape.
   - □ b. die.
   - □ c. break his radio.

3. Across the street from J. T.'s window is a
   - □ a. hospital.
   - □ b. health club.
   - □ c. bar.

4. J. T. left in the middle of the night because he
   - □ a. was running away from home.
   - □ b. needed to get his radio back.
   - □ c. was worried about the cat.

5. J. T.'s mother
   - □ a. feels sorry for the cat.
   - □ b. is allergic to animals.
   - □ c. does not want a cat.

6. The radio helps J. T. feel less
   - □ a. angry.
   - □ b. lonely.
   - □ c. tired.

7. At night J. T.'s neighborhood is
   - □ a. dangerous.
   - □ b. dark.
   - □ c. friendly.

8. Whenever he thinks about the sick cat J. T. is
   - □ a. annoyed.
   - □ b. contented.
   - □ c. worried.

The following passage, taken from the selection you have just read, has words omitted from it. Fill in each blank using a word from the set of five words in the column to the right of the passage. Check your answers using the Answer Key on page 201.

Mama Melcy leaned closer to J. T. and asked, "What you _____ for Christmas, child?" J. T. looked at her for a long time.

"A _____ ," he said. Then, gathering his determination, he continued. "I want me this cat I found. You reckon I could have him? Could I? He needs a _____ . He's real bad off, near dead, almost. Could I?"

A long _____ followed.

His mother got up from the table and scraped the _____ from her plate into the garbage can, then said, "I don't have me enough _____ , I got to nurse me a half-dead cat. Anyhow, only animals they allow in this place is rats."

"But Mama, he's liable to _____ . Please . . . couldn't I keep him? I'm afraid he'll die." J. T. looked anxiously from his _____ to his grandmother.

1. a. getting   b. want   c. hoping
   d. desire   e. buying

2. a. pet   b. animal   c. friend
   d. companion   e. cat

3. a. home   b. bed   c. doctor
   d. meal   e. friend

4. a. hum   b. laugh   c. silence
   d. look   e. dream

5. a. bones   b. dinner   c. hair
   d. leftovers   e. crumbs

6. a. food   b. work   c. jobs
   d. troubles   e. money

7. a. die   b. worsen   c. hurt
   d. expire   e. leave

8. a. cat   b. sister   c. window
   d. mother   e. plate

VOCABULARY

Look at the word in boldface in each exercise that
follows and read carefully the sentence with it. Put an
x in the box before the best meaning or synonym for
the word as it is used in the sentence. Check your
answers using the Answer Key on page 201.

1. Then, gathering his **determination**,
   he continued. "I want me this cat
   I found."
   □ a. strength
   □ b. courage
   □ c. papers

2. "But Mama, he's **liable** to die.
   Please . . . couldn't I keep him?"
   □ a. hoping
   □ b. likely
   □ c. unable

3. J. T. looked **anxiously** from his
   mother to his grandmother.
   □ a. with worry
   □ b. proudly
   □ c. with a laugh

4. "You sure got some **peculiar**
   windows, openin' out onto solid
   brick walls."
   □ a. strange
   □ b. wide
   □ c. painted

5. Popping in uninvited, **flexing** their
   neon muscles. . . .
   □ a. bending
   □ b. noticing
   □ c. weakening

6. . . . throbbing in and out of the room;
   pulsating electronic messages across
   J. T.'s body and over the walls.
   □ a. vibrating
   □ b. whispering
   □ c. catching

7. J. T. stared **blankly** at the lights, unable
   to sleep.
   □ a. with wonder
   □ b. without interest
   □ c. drowsily

8. They had lit a fire in a trash can
   and were **huddled** over it trying to
   keep warm.
   □ a. giggling
   □ b. circling
   □ c. crowding

Set 2

Mystery Monsters of Loch Ness

Patricia Lauber

Reading Time			Maze
Comprehension			Vocabulary

This passage was taken from *Mystery Monsters of Loch Ness* by Patricia Lauber. This book is about the large monster that people have reported seeing in a lake in Scotland. If you would like to read more about the Loch Ness monster, ask your school or local librarian if you can borrow this book.

In the north of Scotland, there is a long, narrow lake. Mountains rise along its sides. Between them, the big lake stretches as far as the eye can see. The water is deep and dark. This is Loch Ness—*loch* is the Scottish word for "lake."

Loch Ness is a lake with a mystery. The mystery goes back hundreds of years. It has to do with a big, strange creature that was said to live in the loch.

Local people believed in this creature. They spoke of it as "the beastie in the loch." Most of the time, they said, the beastie lived under water. But once in a while it came to the surface. Then someone might catch sight of its head or its back or its tail. What was it? No one could say, for no one ever got a good look at it. They thought it must be some kind of fish, since it lived in the loch. But it did not look like any fish they knew.

Before the 1930s, few outsiders had heard of the beastie. Then a road was built along Loch Ness. Many visitors began seeing the loch and hearing about the beastie. Some believed they had caught sight of it.

One of these sightings was written up for a local newspaper. When the editor read the story, he said, "If it's that big, we'll have to call it a monster." That was how the beastie in the loch became the Loch Ness monster. From then on, many papers printed stories about the monster. They made good reading.

These stories made the monster famous. But many readers thought it was a joke. To them, a monster was a make-believe animal, something they might see in a movie. They thought the Scots had invented a monster to draw tourists to the loch.

Accounts of the Loch Ness monster also sounded like jokes. Many people thought they had seen part of it. The parts added up to a very strange creature indeed.

It was said to be 20 or 30 feet long. The body was thick in the middle, but it thinned out toward the ends. There was a long neck with a small head. Some people had seen what looked like horns or feelers—two fleshy stalks that grew out of the head. Some had seen a stiff mane or fin on the neck and shoulders.

Sometimes the back looked like an overturned boat. At other times it had one, two, or three humps. Some people saw two or four flippers. They said the monster swam by paddling with its flippers. Other people saw no flippers. They said it swam by using its powerful tail.

The monster seemed shy. It never

attacked boats or people. It was easily startled by noises, such as the slam of a car door or the putt-putt of an outboard motor. Any noise caused it to disappear. Sometimes the Loch Ness monster sank silently from sight.

COMPREHENSION

Read the following questions and statements. For each one, put an *x* in the box before the option that contains the most complete or accurate answer. Check your answers using the Answer Key on page 202.

1. "Loch" is the Scottish word for
   - ☐ a. scary.
   - ☐ b. monster.
   - ☐ c. lake.

2. What did the local people call the monster in the loch?
   - ☐ a. the big fish
   - ☐ b. the beastie
   - ☐ c. the creature

3. People said that the creature lived most of the time
   - ☐ a. in a cave.
   - ☐ b. under water.
   - ☐ c. in an old boat.

4. People thought the monster was shy because
   - ☐ a. any noise could make it disappear.
   - ☐ b. it blushed easily.
   - ☐ c. it wouldn't speak.

5. How did people who saw the monster describe it?
   - ☐ a. They all agreed it looked like a whale.
   - ☐ b. They all thought it was a dinosaur.
   - ☐ c. They all had different ideas of what it looked like.

6. How did many people feel about the story of the monster?
   - ☐ a. They became afraid.
   - ☐ b. They didn't believe it.
   - ☐ c. They became angry.

7. Probably most people read the newspaper stories about the Loch Ness monster because they were
   - ☐ a. worried.
   - ☐ b. afraid.
   - ☐ c. curious.

8. When people came near the monster, it
   - ☐ a. avoided them.
   - ☐ b. ignored them.
   - ☐ c. chased them away.

The following passage, taken from the selection you have just read, has words omitted from it. Fill in each blank using a word from the set of five words in the column to the right of the passage. Check your answers using the Answer Key on page 202.

In the north of Scotland, there is a long, narrow lake. Mountains rise along its sides. Between them, the big lake stretches as far as the eye can see. The water is _____ 1 and dark. This is Loch Ness—*loch* is the Scottish word for "lake."

Loch Ness is a lake with a _____ 2 . The mystery goes back hundreds of years. It has to do with a big, strange creature that was said to _____ 3 in the loch.

Local people believed in this _____ 4 . They spoke of it as "the beastie in the loch." Most of the time, they said, the beastie lived under _____ 5 . But once in a while it came to the surface. Then someone might catch sight of its head or its back or its _____ 6 . What was it? No one could say, for no one ever got a good _____ 7 at it. They thought it must be some kind of fish, since it lived in the loch. But it did not look like any _____ 8 they knew.

1. a. wet   b. deep   c. shallow
         d. cool   e. warm

2. a. story   b. glow   c. mountain
         d. mystery   e. tale

3. a. live   b. swim   c. stay
         d. sail   e. jump

4. a. lake   b. religion   c. word
         d. ness   e. creature

5. a. water   b. nearby   c. there
         d. wild   e. alone

6. a. foot   b. spikes   c. tail
         d. horns   e. wings

7. a. chance   b. photograph   c. look
         d. view   e. sight

8. a. fish   b. person   c. creature
         d. monster   e. animal

Look at the word in boldface in each exercise that
follows and read carefully the sentence with it. Put an
x in the box before the best meaning or synonym for
the word as it is used in the sentence. Check your
answers using the Answer Key on page 202.

1. They spoke of it as "the **beastie** in
   the loch."
   - ☐ a. mystery
   - ☐ b. creature
   - ☐ c. fish

2. **Local** people believed in this
   creature. . . . Before the 1930s few
   outsiders had heard of the beastie.
   - ☐ a. silly
   - ☐ b. crazy
   - ☐ c. nearby

3. They thought the Scots had invented a
   monster to **draw** tourists to the loch.
   - ☐ a. frighten away
   - ☐ b. paint
   - ☐ c. attract

4. Some people believed they had caught
   sight of it. . . . One of these **sightings**
   was written up for a local newspaper.
   - ☐ a. sounds
   - ☐ b. observations
   - ☐ c. reports

5. **Accounts** of the Loch Ness monster
   also sounded like jokes.
   - ☐ a. stories
   - ☐ b. mysteries
   - ☐ c. flippers

6. They thought the Scots had **invented**
   a monster. . . .
   - ☐ a. built
   - ☐ b. discovered
   - ☐ c. made up

7. The body was thick in the
   middle, but it **thinned out** toward
   the ends.
   - ☐ a. became wider
   - ☐ b. became less thick
   - ☐ c. became thicker

8. Sometimes the back looked like
   an **overturned** boat.
   - ☐ a. upside-down
   - ☐ b. speeding
   - ☐ c. large

The Great Brain at the Academy

John D. Fitzgerald

Reading Time			Maze
Comprehension			Vocabulary

This passage was taken from *The Great Brain at the Academy* by John D. Fitzgerald. It is a story about a boy who is out to outwit everyone at the Catholic Academy for Boys where he is going to school. If you would like to read more of this book, ask for it at your local or school library.

Monday evening at seven twenty-five Tom made his usual announcement. "You fellows are going to have to use the washroom on the second floor for the next half hour."

Then he went inside the washroom and locked the door. He climbed through the trapdoor to the attic and opened the dormer window. In a couple of minutes he saw Daniel coming down the street. Jerry had doubted Daniel would cooperate. But Tom didn't have any doubts after learning Daniel had spent two years at the academy and stood to make fifty cents besides.

Tom let down the string with the rock tied to it. He watched Daniel remove the rock and tie the string to one end of the rope. Then he hauled it up, coiled it on the floor, and returned to the washroom. He did his cleaning job and then joined his three friends on Jerry's bunk.

"Everything went according to plan," he whispered. "Tomorrow you all start earning your ten percent."

"Hold it," Phil said. "I thought I had already earned my ten percent by getting Daniel to buy the rope for you."

"You haven't even started to earn it," Tom said. "Here is the way we will work it. Two of you will go with me to the washroom at seven thirty tomorrow night.

One will have to stay and clean the washroom. The other one will go up to the attic with me to help with the rope. The third can remain in the dormitory. You will each take turns doing the different things that must be done to get the candy store going."

"Count me out," Phil said to Tom's surprise. "We will all get expelled for sure if we get caught smuggling candy into the academy."

Jerry shook his head. "What a worry wart you are," he said with disgust. "We haven't even opened the candy store and already you've got us all expelled."

"I can't help it," Phil said. "This is the only Catholic academy in Utah. And if I get expelled my mother and father will never forgive me."

Tom hadn't expected this. He looked at Tony.

"What about you, Tony?" he asked.

"Haw," Tony said.

"Cut out that haw business," Tom said. "Are you in or out?"

Tony hesitated a moment. "I think Phil is right," he said.

"In that case," Tom said, "would you and Phil mind leaving us? What I have to say is for the ears of stockholders in the corporation only. And Jerry and I will pick two other fellows to become stockholders."

Phil began biting his lip. "You mean we aren't even friends anymore?" he asked.

Jerry spoke before Tom could answer. "Who wants to be friends with a couple of nervous, old worry warts?" he asked.

"Jerry is right," Tom said. "We don't want to have anything to do with a couple of fellows who are going to be worrying all the time about something that can't even happen."

COMPREHENSION

Read the following questions and statements. For each one, put an *x* in the box before the option that contains the most complete or accurate answer. Check your answers using the Answer Key on page 202.

1. Phil is afraid that they will
   - ☐ a. be expelled.
   - ☐ b. lose their money.
   - ☐ c. fall off the rope.

2. What are the boys trying to smuggle into the academy?
   - ☐ a. mice
   - ☐ b. candy
   - ☐ c. kittens

3. According to Phil, what is so special about the academy?
   - ☐ a. It's the only Catholic academy in Utah.
   - ☐ b. It's got the best candy store around.
   - ☐ c. It's got excellent teachers.

4. What does Tom call the boys who take part in his plan?
   - ☐ a. fellow smugglers
   - ☐ b. spoilsports
   - ☐ c. stockholders

5. Tom is probably
   - ☐ a. older than the others.
   - ☐ b. following someone's orders.
   - ☐ c. the leader of the group.

6. Phil's feeling that they might get caught tells us that he is
   - ☐ a. worried.
   - ☐ b. eager.
   - ☐ c. confident.

7. What attitude is Jerry showing toward Phil and Tony when he calls them worry warts?
   - ☐ a. friendly
   - ☐ b. disgusted
   - ☐ c. understanding

8. Why does Phil bite his lip when Tom says he'll find someone else to take his place in the smuggling scheme?
   - ☐ a. He thinks the plan will fail.
   - ☐ b. He's afraid their friendship is over.
   - ☐ c. He feels hungry.

The following passage, taken from the selection you have just read, has words omitted from it. Fill in each blank using a word from the set of five words in the column to the right of the passage. Check your answers using the Answer Key on page 202.

"Count me out," Phil said to Tom's surprise. "We will all get expelled for sure if we get caught smuggling candy into the academy."

Jerry shook his head. "What a worry wart you are," he said with

_____ . "We haven't
                    1
even opened the candy store and already

you've got us _____
                               2
expelled."

"I can't help it," Phil said. "This is the only Catholic academy in Utah. And if I

get _____ my mother
              3
and father will never forgive me."

Tom hadn't expected this. He

_____ at Tony.
                    4
"What about you, Tony?" he asked.

"Haw," Tony said.

"Cut out that haw business," Tom said. "Are you in or out?"

Tony _____ a
                     5
moment. "I think Phil is right," he said.

"In that case," Tom said, "would you

and Phil mind _____
                               6
us? What I have to say is for the ears of

_____ in the
              7

1. a. disgust b. cheerfulness c. sadness

     d. anger e. surprise

2.   a. nearly   b. now   c. both

        d. all   e. almost

3.   a. caught   b. graded   c. expelled

         d. failed   e. suspended

4.   a. frowned   b. winked   c. looked

         d. jumped   e. smiled

5.   a. counted   b. hesitated   c. waited

         d. requested   e. turned

6.   a. joining   b. helping   c. drawing

         d. leaving   e. photographing

7.   a. corn   b. partners   c. pals

         d. stockholders   e. us

corporation only. And Jerry and I will pick two other fellows to become stockholders."

Phil began biting his lip. "You mean we aren't even _____ anymore?" he asked.

8. a. welcomed b. friends c. members

    d. needed e. fellows

VOCABULARY

Look at the word in boldface in each exercise that follows and read carefully the sentence with it. Put an *x* in the box before the best meaning or synonym for the word as it is used in the sentence. Check your answers using the Answer Key on page 202.

1. Monday evening at seven twenty-five Tom made his usual **announcement**.
   - ☐ a. plans
   - ☐ b. speech
   - ☐ c. threat

2. Then he hauled it up, **coiled** it on the floor. . . .
   - ☐ a. threw down
   - ☐ b. rolled up
   - ☐ c. cut up

3. Jerry had doubted Daniel would **cooperate**. But Tom didn't have any doubts. . . .
   - ☐ a. return
   - ☐ b. buy candy
   - ☐ c. help

4. "We will all get **expelled** for sure if we get caught smuggling candy into the academy."
   - ☐ a. forced to leave school
   - ☐ b. given a low grade
   - ☐ c. rewarded

5. "The other one will go up to the attic with me to help with the rope. The third can remain in the **dormitory**."
   - ☐ a. classroom
   - ☐ b. bedroom
   - ☐ c. hallway

6. Jerry shook his head. "What a worry wart you are," he said with **disgust**."
   - ☐ a. praise
   - ☐ b. fear
   - ☐ c. dislike

7. "Are you in or out?" Tony **hesitated** a moment. "I think Phil is right," he said.

☐ a. listened

☐ b. stopped

☐ c. looked around

8. "What I have to say is for the ears of stockholders in the **corporation** only."

☐ a. school

☐ b. academy

☐ c. company

Wilt Chamberlain

Kenneth Rudeen

Reading Time [ ]   [ ] Maze

Comprehension [ ]   [ ] Vocabulary

This passage was taken from the book *Wilt Chamberlain* by Kenneth Rudeen. It is the true story of Wilt Chamberlain, one of the greatest basketball players of all time. If you would like to read more about Wilt, ask for this book at your school or public library.

When a man is taller and stronger than other men, he is sometimes called a giant. Many people think of Wilt Chamberlain as a giant. He is so tall that he has a special, extra-long bed to sleep in and a special car with enough space for his long legs.

When Wilt played basketball, he was one of the most famous basketball players in the world. It is not unusual for a basketball player to be tall. Basketball is a game for the tall and the strong. But Wilt was more than that. There were other players as big as Wilt, but no one else was so skillful at shooting baskets and jumping up high to get rebounds.

During his playing days, Wilt was paid about $200,000 a year. That was what the President of the United States earned for being President. At that time, it was more than any other athlete in the entire history of sports had ever been paid.

Wilt played for the Los Angeles Lakers team. He helped to make it the best team in the Western Division of the National Basketball Association, which is a group of the very finest professional teams in the world.

Wilt owns a beautiful apartment building in Los Angeles, where his mother lives, and another one in New York. He owns racehorses. He wears fine clothes.

He owns an English Bentley car.

But when Wilt was a little boy he probably didn't dream that he would be famous or rich.

Wilton Norman Chamberlain was born August 21, 1936, in West Philadelphia, Pennsylvania. His parents were William and Olivia Chamberlain. William Chamberlain always had a job, but he did not earn much. He was careful not to waste money. He was raising a large family.

Wilt had five brothers and three sisters. That made nine young mouths for William Chamberlain to feed. Nine boys and girls who needed clothes and playthings.

But somehow there was always enough to eat. Olivia Chamberlain was a good cook. She prepared delicious pot roasts, stews, and rice puddings for her family.

To make extra money, Mrs. Chamberlain took in sewing. Mr. Chamberlain worked overtime at his job.

Wilt's father was able to buy a house. He was able to buy a piano, too. The Chamberlain girls took piano lessons for 50 cents apiece. Wilt did not take lessons, but as he grew older he taught himself how to play the piano a little, and how to strum a guitar.

In the streets near his house Wilt played football and baseball with the other boys.

When Wilt was just seven years old, he took a job. He did not tell his mother or father, but one day his mother found out. She looked out into the street and saw Wilt lifting crates for a milkman.

Mrs. Chamberlain told the milkman that Wilt was only seven. She said he shouldn't be lifting those heavy milk crates.

"I thought he was twelve," said the milkman. So Wilt stopped helping the milkman.

COMPREHENSION

Read the following questions and statements. For each one, put an _x_ in the box before the option that contains the most complete or accurate answer. Check your answers using the Answer Key on page 202.

1. According to the story, people sometimes called Wilt Chamberlain a
   ☐ a. giant.
   ☐ b. funny person.
   ☐ c. good guitar player.

2. Wilt earned as much money as the
   ☐ a. head of the F.B.I.
   ☐ b. President of the United States.
   ☐ c. Dodgers' best pitcher.

3. Wilt played for the
   ☐ a. Seattle Seahawks.
   ☐ b. Philadelphia Phillies.
   ☐ c. Los Angeles Lakers.

4. When he was seven years old, Wilt
   ☐ a. took a job.
   ☐ b. learned to play basketball.
   ☐ c. took his first piano lesson.

5. Why was Wilt such a famous basketball player?
   ☐ a. He was from Philadelphia.
   ☐ b. He was very good at the sport.
   ☐ c. He made a lot of money.

6. Was Wilt wealthy as a child?
   ☐ a. No, his parents did not have much money.
   ☐ b. Yes, his parents were very wealthy.
   ☐ c. It's impossible to tell from the story.

7. The fact that Wilt taught himself how to play the piano shows that he
   ☐ a. didn't care about anything except basketball.
   ☐ b. was trying out for a jazz band.
   ☐ c. was eager to learn new things.

8. Which of the words below best describes Wilt at the age of seven?
   ☐ a. independent
   ☐ b. lazy
   ☐ c. frightened

The following passage, taken from the selection you have just read, has words omitted from it. Fill in each blank using a word from the set of five words in the column to the right of the passage. Check your answers using the Answer Key on page 202.

Wilton Norman Chamberlain was born August 21, 1936, in West Philadelphia, Pennsylvania. His _____ 1 were William and Olivia Chamberlain. William Chamberlain always had a _____ 2 , but he did not earn much. He was careful not to waste money. He was raising a large family.

Wilt had five brothers and three _____ 3 . That made nine young mouths for William Chamberlain to feed. Nine boys and girls who needed _____ 4 and playthings.

But somehow there was always enough to _____ 5 . Olivia Chamberlain was a good cook. She prepared delicious pot roasts, stews, and rice puddings for her family.

To make extra _____ 6 , Mrs. Chamberlain took in sewing. Mr. Chamberlain worked overtime at his job.

Wilt's father was able to buy a house. He was able to buy a _____ 7 , too. The Chamberlain girls took piano lessons for 50 cents apiece. Wilt did not

1. a. neighbors b. children c. relatives
   d. grandparents e. parents

2. a. debt b. paycheck c. job
   d. hobby e. business

3. a. sisters b. children c. pets
   d. friends e. brothers

4. a. books b. food c. clothes
   d. shelter e. toys

5. a. survive b. do c. make
   d. eat e. read

6. a. work b. money c. clothes
   d. food e. debt

7. a. guitar b. boat c. piano
   d. television e. car

take _____ , but as he
grew older he taught himself how to play
the piano a little, and how to strum a guitar.

8. a. lessons   b. excuses   c. money
   d. time   e. studies

**Look at the word in boldface in each exercise that
follows and read carefully the sentence with it. Put an
x in the box before the best meaning or synonym for
the word as it is used in the sentence. Check your
answers using the Answer Key on page 202.**

1. It is not **unusual** for a basketball
   player to be tall.
   ☐ a. rare
   ☐ b. often
   ☐ c. unsuitable

2. . . . but no one else was so skillful at
   shooting baskets and jumping up high
   to get **rebounds**.
   ☐ a. points that are won
   ☐ b. balls that roll away
   ☐ c. balls that bounce back

3. He helped to make it the best team in
   the Western **Division** of the National
   Basketball Association. . . .
   ☐ a. group
   ☐ b. team
   ☐ c. state

4. But when Wilt was a little boy, he
   probably didn't dream that he would
   be famous or rich.
   ☐ a. mostly likely
   ☐ b. positively
   ☐ c. usually

5. Mr. Chamberlain worked **overtime**
   at his job.
   ☐ a. extra hours
   ☐ b. occasionally
   ☐ c. very hard

6. He was careful not to **waste** money.
   He was raising a large family.
   ☐ a. spend carefully
   ☐ b. use carelessly
   ☐ c. save carefully

7. He taught himself how to play the
   piano a little, and how to **strum**
   a guitar.
   ☐ a. sing along with
   ☐ b. play the strings of
   ☐ c. decorate

8. The Chamberlain girls took piano
   lessons for 50 cents **apiece**.
   ☐ a. each week
   ☐ b. each lesson
   ☐ c. each day

From the Mixed-Up Files of Mrs. Basil E. Frankweiler

E. L. Konigsburg

Reading Time ☐   ☐ Maze

Comprehension ☐   ☐ Vocabulary

*From the Mixed-Up Files of Mrs. Basil E.
Frankweiler* by E. L. Konigsburg tells about the
adventures of two runaway children and a strange old
woman. If you are interested in reading more of this
book, ask for it at your school or public library.

Claudia had planned her speech. "I want you, Jamie, for the greatest adventure in our lives."

Jamie muttered, "Well, I wouldn't mind if you'd pick on someone else."

Claudia looked out the window and didn't answer. Jamie said, "As long as you've got me here, tell me."

Claudia still said nothing and still looked out the window. Jamie became impatient. "I said that as long as you've got me here, you may as well tell me."

Claudia remained silent. Jamie erupted, "What's the matter with you, Claude? First you bust up my card game, then you don't tell me. It's undecent."

"Break up, not bust up. Indecent, not undecent," Claudia corrected.

"Oh, baloney! You know what I mean. Now tell me," he demanded.

"I've picked you to accompany me on the greatest adventure of our mutual lives," Claudia repeated.

"You said that." He clenched his teeth. "Now tell me."

"I've decided to run away from home, and I've chosen you to accompany me."

"Why pick on me? Why not pick on Steve?" he asked.

Claudia sighed, "I don't want Steve. Steve is one of the things in my life that I'm running away from. I want you."

Despite himself, Jamie felt flattered. (Flattery is as important a machine as the lever, isn't it, Saxonberg? Give it a proper place to rest, and it can move the world.) It moved Jamie. He stopped thinking, "Why pick on me?" and started thinking, "I am chosen." He sat up in his seat, placed his hands over his bent knee, and said out of the corner of his mouth, "O.K., Claude, when do we bust out of here? And how?"

Claudia stifled the urge to correct his grammar again. "On Wednesday. Here's the plan. Listen carefully."

Jamie squinted his eyes and said, "Make it complicated, Claude. I like complications."

Claudia laughed. "It's got to be simple to work. We'll go on Wednesday because Wednesday is music lesson day. I'm taking my violin out of its case and am packing it full of clothes. You do the same with your trumpet case. Take as much clean underwear as possible and socks and at least one other shirt with you."

"All in a trumpet case? I should have taken up the bass fiddle."

"You can use some of the room in my case. Also use your book bag. Take your transistor radio."

"Can I wear sneakers?" Jamie asked.

Claudia answered, "Of course. Wearing

shoes all the time is one of the tyrannies you'll escape by coming with me."

Jamie smiled, and Claudia knew that now was the correct time to ask. She almost managed to sound casual. "And bring all your money." She cleared her throat. "By the way, how much money do you have?"

Jamie put his foot back down on the floor, looked out the window, and said, "Why do you want to know?"

"For goodness' sake, Jamie, if we're in this together, then we're together. I've got to know. How much do you have?"

"Can I trust you not to talk?" he asked. Claudia was getting mad.

COMPREHENSION

Read the following questions and statements. For each one, put an *x* in the box before the option that contains the most complete or accurate answer. Check your answers using the Answer Key on page 202.

1. Claudia is planning
   - ☐ a. a book.
   - ☐ b. an adventure.
   - ☐ c. an argument.

2. Claudia needs help from
   - ☐ a. Steve.
   - ☐ b. Saxonberg.
   - ☐ c. Jamie.

3. Claudia wants to pack their clothing in
   - ☐ a. suitcases.
   - ☐ b. instrument cases.
   - ☐ c. paper bags.

4. Jamie wants to wear
   - ☐ a. clean underwear.
   - ☐ b. sneakers.
   - ☐ c. shoes.

5. Claudia cares about good
   - ☐ a. shoes.
   - ☐ b. grades.
   - ☐ c. grammar.

6. Jamie is
   - ☐ a. in charge of the adventure.
   - ☐ b. interested in the plan.
   - ☐ c. scared to run away from home.

7. Claudia plays the
   - ☐ a. violin.
   - ☐ b. trumpet.
   - ☐ c. trombone.

8. Claudia wants Jamie to go with her because he has
   - ☐ a. a big instrument case.
   - ☐ b. money.
   - ☐ c. many friends.

The following passage, taken from the selection you have just read, has words omitted from it. Fill in each blank using a word from the set of five words in the column to the right of the passage. Check your answers using the Answer Key on page 202.

Claudia had planned her speech. "I want you, Jamie, for the greatest adventure in our lives."

Jamie muttered, "Well, I wouldn't mind if you'd pick on someone else."

Claudia looked out the window and didn't answer. Jamie said, "As long as you've got me here, tell me."

Claudia still said _____ and still looked out the _____ .
Jamie became impatient. "I said that as long as you've got me here, you may as well _____ me."

Claudia remained _____ . Jamie erupted, "What's the matter with you, Claude? First you bust up my card game, then you don't tell me. It's _____ ."

"Break up, not bust up. Indecent, not undecent," Claudia _____ .

"Oh, baloney! You know what I mean. Now tell me," he demanded.

"I've picked you to accompany me on

1. a. speeches   b. plans   c. little
   d. nothing   e. no

2. a. window   b. door   c. space
   d. back   e. view

3.   a. ask   b. hurt   c. tell
   d. find   e. help

4. a. composed b. interested c. uncertain
   d. silent e. behind

5. a. wrong   b. unfair   c. indecent
   d. illegal   e. undecent

6. a. corrected   b. asked   c. wondered
   d. replied   e. stated

the greatest _____ of
our mutual lives," Claudia repeated.

   "You said that." He clenched his teeth.
"Now tell me."

   "I've decided to run away from home,
and I've chosen you to

_____ me."

7.   a. trip   b. journey   c. adventure

                d. hope   e. time

8.   a. help   b. watch   c. pay

            d. accompany   e. find

VOCABULARY

**Look at the word in boldface in each exercise that
follows and read carefully the sentence with it. Put an
x in the box before the best meaning or synonym for
the word as it is used in the sentence. Check your
answers using the Answer Key on page 202.**

1. Jamie **erupted**, "What's the matter
with you, Claude?"
- □ a. burst out
- □ b. whispered
- □ c. repeated

2. "I've picked you to accompany me on
the greatest adventure of our **mutual**
lives," Claudia repeated.
- □ a. adult
- □ b. separate
- □ c. shared

3. He **clenched** his teeth. "Now
tell me."
- □ a. cleaned
- □ b. closed tightly
- □ c. chewed loudly

4. "I've decided to run away from home,
and I've chosen you to **accompany** me."
- □ a. stay away from
- □ b. come with
- □ c. imagine

5. Claudia **stifled** the urge to correct his
grammar again.
- □ a. smothered
- □ b. encouraged
- □ c. continued

6. Jamie **squinted** his eyes and said,
"Make it complicated, Claude. I like
complications."
- □ a. blinked rapidly
- □ b. widened
- □ c. partially closed

7. "Wearing shoes all the time is one of the **tyrannies** you'll escape by coming with me."
   - ☐ a. rules
   - ☐ b. chores
   - ☐ c. secrets

8. . . . Claudia knew that now was the correct time to ask. She almost managed to sound **casual**.
   - ☐ a. formal
   - ☐ b. wise
   - ☐ c. unconcerned

The World of Robots

Jonathan Rutland

Reading Time	⬜ ⬜	Maze
Comprehension	⬜ ⬜	Vocabulary

This passage was taken from *The World of Robots* by
Jonathan Rutland. It is the story of what robots are
and how they help us. If you enjoy this passage and
would like to read more about robots, ask for the
book at either your school or public library.

There are robots all around us. Some do very complicated jobs like flying airplanes and driving subway trains. And some do one simple job.

When an automatic washing machine is switched on, water pours in. The machine waits until the water is hot before washing the clothes. It does this by "feedback." Information about what is happening is "fed back" into the robot. This information tells it what to do next.

Our eyes, ears, and other senses are our feedback. They tell us what is going on around us. Robots are like people, then, in two ways. They work and they have feedback.

But very few robots look like people. Many are hidden away. Robots control the temperature of our houses, our cookers, our hot water systems. We can set the controls to the temperature we want. The robot does the rest. Its feedback usually comes from a thermostat.

One kind of thermostat is a strip of metal which bends when it gets hot. At the right temperature, it bends just enough to work a switch. This turns off the heat. As the air around it cools, the metal straightens, and this turns the heat on again.

There are robots all around, making our lives easier. Some of them, like the pocket calculator, can work much more quickly than human beings can. And they rarely make mistakes.

In some ways robots are better than people. They work quickly, but do not make mistakes. They do not get bored doing the same job over and over again. And they never get tired.

So robots are very useful in factories. They can be taught to do many different jobs. First their electronic brains must be shown how the job is done. A person moves the robot's "arms" and "hand" through each part of the job. The robot's brain remembers each move. When the robot is put to work on its own, its brain controls the rods, wheels, and motors which move its arm.

When the robot is needed for a new job, its electronic memory is "wiped clean." Then it is taught how to do its new task.

If the robot's hand stops working, or if something gets in the way, it cannot do the next part of the job. So it stops and signals for help. Then a human engineer attends to the fault.

Robots are also used for doing jobs that are dangerous. They can move objects that are too hot or too heavy for people to handle. They can work in places that are too hot or too cold for people. And they are not affected by poisonous fumes or gases.

The most "intelligent" robots can move and see. Their eyes are cameras. Their metal fingers can feel shapes. They can find out how hot or cold objects are.

These robots have computer brains, linked to their eyes and fingers. Their brains control their actions.

These expensive robots are used in scientific research. They do such jobs as handling radioactive materials.

COMPREHENSION

Read the following questions and statements. For each one, put an _x_ in the box before the option that contains the most complete or accurate answer. Check your answers using the Answer Key on page 202.

1. In this article the author tells us that
   - ☐ a. there are very few robots.
   - ☐ b. we see robots only at certain times.
   - ☐ c. robots are all around us.

2. In this article we are told that
   - ☐ a. we get feedback through our eyes and ears.
   - ☐ b. we get feedback through the robots.
   - ☐ c. only robots get feedback.

3. The author says that in factories robots
   - ☐ a. only get in the way.
   - ☐ b. break down a lot.
   - ☐ c. are very useful.

4. The robots used for scientific research are
   - ☐ a. not very "intelligent."
   - ☐ b. very expensive.
   - ☐ c. very cheap.

5. People keep making robots because robots
   - ☐ a. are fun.
   - ☐ b. are useful.
   - ☐ c. make nice pets.

6. The fact that a robot never gets bored doing the same job over and over again probably means that it
   - ☐ a. will do some jobs better than people.
   - ☐ b. will not do anything better than people.
   - ☐ c. is very like people.

7. In the future, scientists will probably
   - ☐ a. build better robots.
   - ☐ b. stop making robots.
   - ☐ c. no longer be necessary.

8. The author has written a
   - ☐ a. humorous article.
   - ☐ b. sad story.
   - ☐ c. informative article.

The following passage, taken from the selection you have just read, has words omitted from it. Fill in each blank using a word from the set of five words in the column to the right of the passage. Check your answers using the Answer Key on page 202.

When the robot is needed for a new job, its electronic memory is "wiped clean." Then it is taught how to do its _____ task.
1

If the robot's hand stops working, or if something gets in the way, it cannot do the next part of the job. So it stops and signals for _____ .
2
Then a human engineer attends to the fault.

Robots are also used for doing jobs that are dangerous. They can move _____ that are too hot
3
or too heavy for people to handle. They can work in places that are too hot or too cold for _____ . And
4
they are not affected by poisonous fumes or gases.

The most "intelligent" robots can move and _____ . Their eyes
5
are cameras. Their metal fingers can feel shapes. They can find out how _____ or cold objects
6
are. These robots have computer brains, linked to their eyes and fingers. Their brains _____ their
7
actions.

1. a. electric   b. clean   c. new
    d. difficult   e. human

2. a. attention b. directions c. electricity
    d. cleaning e. help

3. a. objects   b. robots   c. gases
    d. metal   e. liquids

4. a. weather   b. people   c. signals
    d. working   e. computer

5. a. stop   b. act   c. think
    d. see   e. photograph

6. a. heavy   b. thick   c. hot
    d. dangerous   e. electronic

7. a. control   b. data   c. decide
    d. design   e. link

These expensive robots are used in _____ research. They do such jobs as handling radioactive materials.

8.

8. a. written   b. robotic   c. scientific
   d. medical   e. weather

VOCABULARY

Look at the word in boldface in each exercise that follows and read carefully the sentence with it. Put an *x* in the box before the best meaning or synonym for the word as it is used in the sentence. Check your answers using the Answer Key on page 202.

1. Some do very **complicated** jobs like flying airplanes and driving subway trains.
   - ☐ a. easy
   - ☐ b. simple
   - ☐ c. difficult

2. **Information** about what is happening is "fed back" into the robot.
   - ☐ a. temperature
   - ☐ b. controls
   - ☐ c. facts

3. Robots control the **temperature** of our houses, our cookers. . . .
   - ☐ a. air flow
   - ☐ b. heating and cooling
   - ☐ c. lighting

4. When an **automatic** washing machine is switched on, water pours in. The machine waits until the water is hot before washing the clothes.
   - ☐ a. expensive
   - ☐ b. self-controlled
   - ☐ c. electronic

5. Our eyes, ears, and other senses are our **feedback**. They tell us what is going on around us.
   - ☐ a. nerves
   - ☐ b. senses
   - ☐ c. source of facts

6. One kind of **thermostat** is a strip of metal which bends when it gets hot.
   - ☐ a. thermometer
   - ☐ b. a device that controls temperature
   - ☐ c. a container for hot drinks

7. . . . if something gets in the way, it cannot do the next part of the job. So it stops and **signals** for help.
   - ☐ a. gives a sign
   - ☐ b. whistles
   - ☐ c. flashes a light

8. Then a human engineer **attends** to the fault.
   - ☐ a. records
   - ☐ b. takes care of
   - ☐ c. observes

Set 3

Mom, You're Fired!

Nancy K. Robinson

Reading Time ☐   ☐ Maze

Comprehension ☐   ☐ Vocabulary

Mom, You're Fired! by Nancy K. Robinson
is a book about two children trying to cope
with their embarrassing mother. If you are
interested in reading more of this book,
ask for it at your school or local library.

Is this the bus to Davenport Street?"
Tina's mother called up to the bus driver,
but he didn't seem to hear her.

Tina's mother stepped up onto the bus.
She was carrying two shopping bags
under one arm and Tina's little sister
Angela under the other arm. Angela
twisted around until she was almost
hanging upside down.

"New shoes," said Angela to the man
in back of her, pointing proudly to her
new white shoes. "Much too esspensive,"
she added.

Tina and her brother Nathaniel looked
at each other. Then they stepped back in
line and let two ladies get in front of
them. They each had their own bus fare
and wanted to get as far away from their
mother and little sister as possible.

They heard their mother ask in an even
louder voice:

"Driver, I asked if this was the bus to
Davenport Street."

"Read the sign, lady," they heard the
bus driver shout.

"The sign outside is stuck," their
mother said crossly.

There was no answer from the bus
driver.

"Hurry up, lady," called a man at the
end of the line.

Their mother wasn't in any hurry. She
was giving the bus driver a lecture.

". . . and the least you could do
is tell me whether or not I'm on the
right bus. It would only be common
courtesy . . ."

"Oh, no." Nathaniel grabbed Tina's
arm. "Here she goes again." He pulled
Tina back and let a boy carrying a large
transistor radio get in front of them.

"Look lady," hollered the bus driver.
"Are you getting on or off? I don't have
all day."

Everyone in line was very quiet.

Tina stared hard at a crack in the sidewalk. She felt like pulling her mother off
the bus and shaking her.

"Move it, lady," the man at the back of
the line called again.

"It's the right bus," a lady called out.
"It's a number 8. This one goes to
Davenport Street."

"Thank you." Tina's mother turned
around and nodded to the lady. "But I
don't see why the bus driver couldn't have
told me that. If I had a choice, I wouldn't
even take this bus."

Nathaniel groaned. "Why can't she just
get on the bus and be quiet like everyone
else?"

Slowly the line of people began to
move ahead.

"Nathaniel, Christina, are you there?"

Now their mother was inside the bus, pounding on the window and waving at them. Tina and Nathaniel pretended not to notice.

As they were paying their fare, they saw a man get up and give their mother his seat. Tina and Nathaniel tried to squeeze to the rear of the bus, but it was too crowded to move. They were stuck right across the aisle from their mother, who had Angela on her lap.

"New shoes," said Angela to everyone who passed by.

Nathaniel grabbed onto a pole and began to read an advertisement posted above the window.

YOU TOO CAN BE A
NATURAL BLONDE OR REDHEAD

COMPREHENSION

Read the following questions and statements. For each one, put an *x* in the box before the option that contains the most complete or accurate answer. Check your answers using the Answer Key on page 203.

1. Tina and her family were trying to get to
   ☐ a. the shopping area.
   ☐ b. the back of the bus.
   ☐ c. Davenport Street.

2. Tina and Nathaniel let two ladies get in front of them because they wanted to
   ☐ a. pay the bus fare like adults.
   ☐ b. get away from their mother.
   ☐ c. be polite.

3. Nathaniel wished that
   ☐ a. the number 8 bus would be late.
   ☐ b. the boy with the radio would let him get in front.
   ☐ c. his mother would be silent.

4. As their mother waved to them from the window, Tina and Nathaniel
   ☐ a. waved good-bye.
   ☐ b. slowly paid the bus driver.
   ☐ c. pretended not to see her.

5. Tina's mother had to shout at the bus driver because
   ☐ a. she was too far back in the line.
   ☐ b. he could not hear with the motor running.
   ☐ c. he was ignoring her.

6. The best word to describe Tina and Nathaniel's feelings is
   ☐ a. embarrassment.
   ☐ b. calm.
   ☐ c. angry.

7. Angela said the shoes were "much too esspensive" because she
   - ☐ a. had to save her allowance to buy them.
   - ☐ b. wanted to let the man know she was very rich.
   - ☐ c. probably heard her mother say how expensive they were.

8. Nathaniel read the advertisement because he
   - ☐ a. could pretend he was not paying attention to his mother.
   - ☐ b. had to practice reading every day.
   - ☐ c. was interested in coloring his hair.

MAZE

The following passage, taken from the selection you have just read, has words omitted from it. Fill in each blank using a word from the set of five words in the column to the right of the passage. Check your answers using the Answer Key on page 203.

Tina's mother stepped up onto the bus. She was carrying two _____ bags under one arm and Tina's little sister Angela under the other arm. Angela twisted around until she was almost _____ upside down.

"New shoes," said Angela to the man in back of her, pointing proudly to her new white shoes. "Much too esspensive," she added.

Tina and her _____ Nathaniel looked at each other. Then they stepped back in line and let two ladies get in front of them. They each had their own bus fare and wanted to get as far away from their mother and _____ sister as possible.

1. a. grocery   b. heavy   c. shopping
   d. overflowing   e. brown

2. a. hanging   b. swinging   c. folded
   d. awkwardly   e. flying

3. a. brother   b. neighbor   c. friend
   d. cousin   e. uncle

4. a. older   b. loud   c. nasty
   d. bossy   e. little

They heard their mother ask in an even louder voice:

"Driver, I asked if this was the _____ to Davenport Street."

"Read the _____, lady," they heard the bus driver shout.

"The sign outside is _____," their mother said crossly.

There was no answer from the bus driver.

"Hurry up, lady," called a man at the end of the _____ .

5. a. way   b. road   c. line
    d. bus   e. subway

6. a. notice   b. sign   c. paper
    d. poster   e. flyer

7. a. missing b. stuck   c. backwards
    d. off   e. broken

8. a. bus   b. crowd   c. day
    d. line   e. street

VOCABULARY

Look at the word in boldface in each exercise that follows and read carefully the sentence with it. Put an x in the box before the best meaning or synonym for the word as it is used in the sentence. Check your answers using the Answer Key on page 203.

1. Angela **twisted** around until she was almost hanging upside down.
   - ☐ a. turned
   - ☐ b. flew
   - ☐ c. jumped

2. "New shoes," said Angela to the man in back of her, pointing **proudly** to her new white shoes.
   - ☐ a. straight towards
   - ☐ b. very pleased
   - ☐ c. shyly

3. They each had their own bus **fare** and wanted to get as far away from their mother and little sister as possible.
   - ☐ a. money
   - ☐ b. seat
   - ☐ c. route

4. "The sign outside is stuck," said their mother **crossly.**
   - ☐ a. angrily
   - ☐ b. excitedly
   - ☐ c. fearfully

5. She was giving the bus driver a **lecture**. ". . . and the least you could do is tell me whether or not I'm on the right bus."
   ☐ a. a snack
   ☐ b. a talk
   ☐ c. a token

6. "Look, lady," **hollered** the bus driver.
   ☐ a. reached out
   ☐ b. announced
   ☐ c. shouted

7. Nathaniel **groaned**. "Why can't she just get on the bus and be quiet like everyone else?"
   ☐ a. moaned
   ☐ b. greeted
   ☐ c. grew

8. Nathaniel grabbed onto a pole and began to read an **advertisement** posted above a window.
   ☐ a. a public notice
   ☐ b. a free newspaper
   ☐ c. a book jacket

We Live in Mexico

Carlos Somonte

This passage is from *We Live in Mexico* by Carlos Somonte. It describes a boy growing up in a Mexican fishing village who has many dreams about the future. If you are interested in reading more of this book, ask for it at your school or public library.

My father taught me to swim when I was two years old and I could fish by the time I was five. And now these two activities, along with exploring, are my favorite pastimes. My village, Paraiso Escondido, has water all round it. The Pacific Ocean laps onto the beach where the village is situated. There's a wide river just inland a short way, with palm trees and mangroves on its banks. So you can see that there's plenty of opportunity for me to do what I like to do most.

My village is not large enough to have a school. Only fifty families live here. So I have to travel every day, from Monday to Friday, to a nearby town for my classes. The school hours are from 8 A.M. to 2 P.M. To get there on time I have to leave the village by 7 A.M. I then get in my *cayuco*—a small wooden boat which I propel with a wooden pole—and cross the river, before walking 3 km (2 miles) to the school.

My school is an elementary school. The children here are between the ages of six and twelve. Some towns also have nursery schools for younger children, but in many rural areas these don't exist. When I'm thirteen I'll be going on to secondary school where my education will last for three years. And if I do well in my exams, I can then decide whether I should go on to high school and then to a college or perhaps to a university, or leave the educational system altogether and become a fisherman like my father. If I go on to higher education, I wouldn't finish being a student until I was twenty-four!

At school I learn Spanish—Mexico's official language—mathematics, geography, and history. But my favorite class is phys. ed. when we play football or basketball. I don't get much homework at the moment, perhaps only an hour or two to do each week, but in a year's time I expect this to increase.

When I'm on vacation, I like to get up early and explore the river in my *cayuco*. I always take with me a fishing line and some bait to catch catfish and some small traps called *jaiberos* for catching crabs. And with my net I catch river shrimps which Mom always likes to put in her tasty broth. I also like to climb the trees along the river banks and jump from the branches into the water.

I like living here and am looking forward to the day very soon when I can join my father fishing in the open sea from his motor boat. Then I might be able to catch a very big fish, such as a shark or barracuda! But first I need to gain some weight and grow a bit taller. Until then I'll practice fishing for catfish and other fish in the river where it's safe.

COMPREHENSION

Read the following questions and statements. For each one, put an *x* in the box before the option that contains the most complete or accurate answer. Check your answers using the Answer Key on page 203.

1. When he was five years old the boy learned to
   □ a. swim.
   □ b. fish.
   □ c. explore.

2. At what time does he leave for school?
   □ a. 7 A.M.
   □ b. 8 A.M.
   □ c. 3 P.M.

3. A *cayuco* is a
   □ a. type of fishing pole.
   □ b. trap for catching crabs.
   □ c. boat made of wood.

4. When he's on vacation, the boy likes to
   □ a. catch river shrimp.
   □ b. fish in the sea.
   □ c. play basketball.

5. The boy has learned many skills from his
   □ a. father.
   □ b. mother.
   □ c. grandmother.

6. Many people in the village earn a living from
   □ a. entertaining tourists.
   □ b. teaching nursery school.
   □ c. fishing in the ocean.

7. After the boy gets heavier and taller, he will be able to
   □ a. start going to school.
   □ b. fish for river shrimps.
   □ c. fish on the open sea.

8. You can conclude that the boy
   □ a. is proud of his life.
   □ b. cannot wait to move away.
   □ c. will need to go to school in order to be a fisherman.

MAZE

The following passage, taken from the selection you have just read, has words omitted from it. Fill in each blank using a word from the set of five words in the column to the right of the passage. Check your answers using the Answer Key on page 203.

My _____ , Paraiso Escondido, has water all around it. The

1. a. land   b. area   c. village
       d. beach   e. home

Pacific Ocean laps onto the beach where the village is situated. There's a wide _____ just inland a short way, with palm trees and mangroves on its banks. So you can see that there's plenty of opportunity for me to do what I like to do most.

My village is not large enough to have a _____ . Only fifty families live here. So I have to travel every day, from Monday to Friday, to a nearby town for my classes. The school _____ are from 8 A.M. to 2 P.M. To get there on time I have to leave the village by 7 A.M. I then get in my *cayuco*—a small wooden _____ which I propel with a wooden pole—and cross the river, before walking 3 km (2 miles) to the school.

My school is an elementary school. The _____ here are between the ages of six and twelve. Some towns also have _____ schools for younger children, but in many rural areas these don't exist. When I'm thirteen I'll be going on to secondary school where my _____ will last for three years.

2. a. river   b. boulevard   c. highway
    d. lake   e. desert

3. a. bus   b. government   c. school
    d. teacher   e. college

4. a. opens   b. closes   c. times
    d. hours   e. schedule

5. a. paddle   b. bridge   c. dock
    d. boat   e. ship

6. a. children   b. books   c. teachers
    d. buildings   e. lessons

7. a. smaller   b. better   c. nursery
    d. learning   e. reading

8. a. exams   b. finals   c. travel
    d. schedule   e. education

Look at the word in boldface in each exercise that follows and read carefully the sentence with it. Put an *x* in the box before the best meaning or synonym for the word as it is used in the sentence. Check your answers using the Answer Key on page 203.

1. And now these two activities, along with exploring, are my favorite **pastimes.**
   - ☐ a. free-time fun
   - ☐ b. daily chores
   - ☐ c. childhood memories

2. The Pacific Ocean **laps** onto the beach where the village is situated.
   - ☐ a. folds up tightly
   - ☐ b. washes gently
   - ☐ c. sits without moving

3. So you can see there's plenty of **opportunity** for me to do what I like to do most.
   - ☐ a. freedom
   - ☐ b. chances
   - ☐ c. opinions

4. I then get in my cayuco—a small wooden boat which I **propel** with a wooden pole. . . .
   - ☐ a. steer
   - ☐ b. fly
   - ☐ c. sink

5. Some towns also have nursery schools for younger children, but in many **rural** areas these don't exist.
   - ☐ a. country
   - ☐ b. city
   - ☐ c. traffic-filled

6. At school I learn Spanish—Mexico's **official** language . . .
   - ☐ a. difficult to learn
   - ☐ b. no longer spoken
   - ☐ c. used by the government

7. When I'm on vacation I like to get up early and **explore** the river in my *cayuco.*
   - ☐ a. fish in
   - ☐ b. swim and play in
   - ☐ c. search and discover in

8. And with my net I catch river shrimps which Mom likes to put in her **tasty** broth.
   - ☐ a. good-tasting
   - ☐ b. sour
   - ☐ c. well-aged

Pippi Longstocking

Astrid Lindgren

Reading Time			Maze
Comprehension			Vocabulary

The following passage was taken from *Pippi Longstocking* by Astrid Lindgren. It is a story about a girl who lives by herself because her mother has died and her father has been lost at sea. If you would like to read more about Pippi, ask for the book at either your school or public library.

Annika woke up early the next morning. She jumped out of bed and ran over to Tommy.

"Wake up, Tommy," she cried, pulling him by the arm. "Wake up and let's go see that funny girl with the big shoes."

Tommy was wide awake in an instant.

"I knew, even while I was sleeping, that something exciting was going to happen today, but I didn't remember what it was," he said as he yanked off his pajama jacket. Off they went to the bathroom, washed themselves and brushed their teeth much faster than usual, had their clothes on in a twinkling, and a whole hour before their mother expected them came sliding down the bannister and landed at the breakfast table. Down they sat and announced that they wanted their hot chocolate right at that very moment.

"What's going to happen today that you're in such a hurry?" asked their mother.

"We're going to see the new girl next door," said Tommy.

"We may stay all day," said Annika.

That morning Pippi was busy making *pepparkakor*—a kind of Swedish cookie. She had made an enormous amount of dough and rolled it out on the kitchen floor.

"Because," said Pippi to her little monkey, "what earthly use is a baking board when one plans to make at least five hundred cookies?"

And there she lay on the floor, cutting out cookie hearts for dear life.

"Stop climbing around in the dough, Mr. Nilsson," she said crossly just as the doorbell rang.

Pippi ran and opened the door. She was white as a miller from top to toe, and when she shook hands heartily with Tommy and Annika a whole cloud of flour blew over them.

"So nice you called," she said and shook her apron—so there came another cloud of flour. Tommy and Annika got so much in their throats that they could not help coughing.

"What are you doing?" asked Tommy.

"Well, if I say that I'm sweeping the chimney, you won't believe me, you're so clever," said Pippi. "Fact is, I'm baking. But I'll soon be done. You can sit on the woodbox for a while."

Pippi could work fast, she could. Tommy and Annika sat and watched how she went through the dough, how she threw the cookies onto the cookie pans, and swung the pans into the oven. They thought it was as good as a circus.

"Done!" said Pippi at last and shut

the oven door on the last pans with a bang.

"What are we going to do now?" asked Tommy.

"I don't know what you are going to do," said Pippi, "but I know I can't lie around and be lazy. I am a Thing-Finder, and when you're a Thing-Finder you don't have a minute to spare."

"What did you say you are?" asked Annika.

"A Thing-Finder."

"What's that?" asked Tommy.

"Somebody who hunts for things, naturally. What else could it be?" said Pippi, sweeping up the flour.

COMPREHENSION

Read the following questions and statements. For each one, put an *x* in the box before the option that contains the most complete or accurate answer. Check your answers using the Answer Key on page 203.

1. Annika and Tommy were in a hurry that morning so they could
   - ☐ a. see Pippi.
   - ☐ b. surprise their mother.
   - ☐ c. drink their hot chocolate.

2. What was Pippi busy doing on the same morning?
   - ☐ a. cleaning the oven
   - ☐ b. sweeping out the chimney
   - ☐ c. making cookies

3. What did Tommy and Annika think was as much fun as the circus?
   - ☐ a. eating Pippi's cookies
   - ☐ b. watching Pippi work
   - ☐ c. playing with Pippi's monkey

4. On that day Pippi was planning to
   - ☐ a. bathe her monkey.
   - ☐ b. go to the circus.
   - ☐ c. hunt for things.

5. How do Tommy and Annika feel about Pippi?
   - ☐ a. They like her very much.
   - ☐ b. They are angry with her.
   - ☐ c. They don't want to see her anymore.

6. Tommy and Annika visit Pippi because
   - ☐ a. their mother wants them to.
   - ☐ b. she does such exciting things.
   - ☐ c. she makes the best cookies.

7. Pippi always wants to be
   - ☐ a. doing something.
   - ☐ b. reading a book.
   - ☐ c. sleeping.

8. Who would you say is the leader amongst the three children?
   - ☐ a. Tommy
   - ☐ b. Annika
   - ☐ c. Pippi

MAZE

The following passage, taken from the selection you have just read, has words omitted from it. Fill in each blank using a word from the set of five words in the column to the right of the passage. Check your answers using the Answer Key on page 203.

That morning Pippi was busy making *pepparkakor*—a kind of Swedish _____ . She had made
1
an enormous amount of dough and rolled it out on the kitchen

_____ .
2

"Because," said Pippi to her little monkey, "what earthly use is a baking board when one plans to make at least five hundred cookies?"

And there she lay on the floor,

_____ out cookie
3
hearts for dear life.

"Stop climbing around in the dough, Mr. Nilsson," she said crossly just as the doorbell rang.

Pippi ran and opened the

_____ . She was
4
white as a miller from top to toe, and when she shook hands heartily with Tommy and Annika a whole cloud of

_____ blew over them.
5
"So nice you called," she said and shook her apron—so there came another

_____ of flour.
6
Tommy and Annika got so much in their

1. a. tea   b. treat   c. bread
    d. cookie   e. cake

2. a. floor   b. table   c. counter
    d. rug   e. mat

3. a. baking   b. tracing   c. cutting
    d. pulling   e. searching

4. a. bell   b. window   c. cupboard
    d. screen   e. door

5. a. flour   b. rain   c. wind
    d. dough   e. tears

6. a. pinch   b. sprinkling   c. drop
    d. cloud   e. roll

throats that they could not help

_____ .
                7

"What are you doing?" asked Tommy.

"Well, if I say that I'm sweeping the chimney, you won't believe me, you're so clever," said Pippi. "Fact is, I'm

_____ . But I'll soon
                8

be done."

7. a. coughing b. laughing c. sneezing

     d. choking e. crying

8. a. cooking b. waiting c. sweeping

     d. cutting e. baking

VOCABULARY

Look at the word in boldface in each exercise that follows and read carefully the sentence with it. Put an *x* in the box before the best meaning or synonym for the word as it is used in the sentence. Check your answers using the Answer Key on page 203.

1. Tommy was wide awake in an instant. . . . He **yanked** off his pajama jacket.
   - ☐ a. cut
   - ☐ b. jerked
   - ☐ c. unbuttoned

2. . . . they brushed their teeth much faster than usual, had their clothes on in a **twinkling**. . . .
   - ☐ a. a very short time
   - ☐ b. an hour
   - ☐ c. twenty minutes

3. . . . they came sliding down the **bannister** and landed at the breakfast table.
   - ☐ a. fireman's pole
   - ☐ b. railing of a stair
   - ☐ c. playground slide

4. Down they sat and **announced** that they wanted their hot chocolate right at that very moment.
   - ☐ a. spoke firmly
   - ☐ b. wrote politely
   - ☐ c. asked proudly

5. She had made an **enormous** amount of dough and rolled it out on the kitchen floor.
   - ☐ a. very small
   - ☐ b. very large
   - ☐ c. very thin

6. ". . . what **earthly** use is a baking board when one plans to make at least five hundred cookies?"
   - ☐ a. wonderful
   - ☐ b. muddy
   - ☐ c. possible

7. . . . when she shook hands **heartily** with Tommy and Annika a whole cloud of flour blew over them.
   - ☐ a. firmly and strongly
   - ☐ b. weakly and slowly
   - ☐ c. quickly

8. ". . . when you're a Thing-Finder you don't have a minute to **spare**."
   - ☐ a. push over
   - ☐ b. give away
   - ☐ c. waste

James and the Giant Peach

Roald Dahl

Reading Time [ ]   [ ] Maze

Comprehension [ ]   [ ] Vocabulary

This passage is from *James and the Giant Peach* by Roald Dahl. It tells the story of a boy who meets some very odd creatures inside the pit of a giant peach. If you are interested in reading more of this book, ask for it at your school or public library.

Lights out," said the Centipede drowsily. Nothing happened.

"Turn out the light!" he called, raising his voice.

James glanced round the room, wondering which of the others he might be talking to, but they were all asleep. The Old-Green-Grasshopper was snoring loudly though his nose. The Ladybug was making whistling noises as she breathed, and the Earthworm was coiled up like a spring at one end of his hammock, wheezing and blowing through his open mouth. As for Miss Spider, she had made a lovely web for herself across one corner of the room, and James could see her crouching right in the very center of it, mumbling softly in her dreams.

"I said turn out the light!" shouted the Centipede angrily.

"Are you talking to me?" James asked him.

"Of course I'm not talking to you," the Centipede answered. "That crazy Glow-worm has gone to sleep with her light on!"

For the first time since entering the room, James glanced up at the ceiling— and there he saw a most extraordinary sight. Something that looked like a gigantic fly without wings was standing upside down upon its six legs in the middle of the ceiling, and the tail end of this creature seemed to be literally on fire. A brilliant greenish light as bright as the brightest electric bulb was shining out of its tail and lighting up the whole room.

"Is *that* a Glow-worm?" asked James, staring at the light. "It doesn't look like a worm of any sort to me."

"Of course it's a Glow-worm," the Centipede answered. "At least that's what *she* calls herself. Although actually you are quite right. She isn't really a worm at all. Glow-worms are never worms. They are simply lady fireflies without wings. Wake up, you lazy beast!"

But the Glow-worm didn't stir, so the Centipede reached out of his hammock and picked up one of his boots from the floor. "Put out that wretched light!" he shouted, hurling the boot up at the ceiling.

The Glow-worm slowly opened one eye and stared at the Centipede. "There is no need to be rude," she said coldly. "All in good time."

"Come on!" shouted the Centipede. "Or I'll put it out for you!"

"Oh, hello, James!" the Glow-worm said, looking down and giving James a little wave and a smile. "I didn't see you come in. Welcome my dear boy, welcome—and goodnight!"

Then *click*—and out went the light.

James Henry Trotter lay there in the darkness with his eyes wide open, listening to the strange sleeping noises that the "creatures" were making all around him, and wondering what on earth was going to happen to him in the morning. Already, he was beginning to like his new friends very much. They were not nearly as terrible as they looked. In fact, they weren't really terrible at all. They seemed extremely kind and helpful in spite of all the shouting and arguing that went on between them.

"Good night," he whispered.

COMPREHENSION

Read the following questions and statements. For each one, put an *x* in the box before the option that contains the most complete or accurate answer. Check your answers using the Answer Key on page 203.

1. When the Centipede first asked that the lights be turned off,
   - ☐ a. everyone jumped.
   - ☐ b. no one moved.
   - ☐ c. James turned off the light.

2. Who was making the whistling sound?
   - ☐ a. the Old-Green-Grasshopper
   - ☐ b. the Ladybug
   - ☐ c. the Firefly

3. The creature with the bright light was the
   - ☐ a. Centipede.
   - ☐ b. Earthworm.
   - ☐ c. Glow-worm.

4. James thinks that the insects are
   - ☐ a. kind and friendly.
   - ☐ b. quiet and shy.
   - ☐ c. frightening and cruel.

5. The Glow-worm annoys
   - ☐ a. James.
   - ☐ b. the Old-Green-Grasshopper.
   - ☐ c. the Centipede.

6. The story takes place during
   - ☐ a. the daytime.
   - ☐ b. the nighttime.
   - ☐ c. dinnertime.

7. James lies awake because he is
   - ☐ a. scared.
   - ☐ b. curious.
   - ☐ c. leaving soon.

8. James has
   - ☐ a. recently met these insects.
   - ☐ b. known all the insects for a long time.
   - ☐ c. known the Glow-worm for a long time.

MAZE

The following passage, taken from the selection you have just read, has words omitted from it. Fill in each blank using a word from the set of five words in the column to the right of the passage. Check your answers using the Answer Key on page 203.

"Turn out the light!" he called, raising his _____1_____ .

James glanced round the room, wondering which of the others he might be talking to, but they were all _____2_____ . The Old-Green-Grasshopper was snoring loudly though his nose. The Ladybug was making whistling _____3_____ as she breathed, and the Earthworm was coiled up like a spring at one end of his hammock, wheezing and blowing through his open _____4_____ . As for Miss Spider, she had made a lovely _____5_____ for herself across one corner of the room, and James could see her crouching right in the very center of it, mumbling softly in her dreams.

"I said turn out the _____6_____ !" shouted the Centipede angrily.

"Are you talking to me?" James asked him.

"Of course I'm not talking to you," the _____7_____ answered.

1. a. arm   b. head   c. voice
    d. lamp   e. eyebrow

2. a. quiet   b. laughing   c. gone
    d. busy   e. asleep

3. a. breaths   b. sounds   c. songs
    d. noises   e. music

4. a. flap   b. nose   c. door
    d. mouth   e. gill

5. a. web   b. spot   c. tent
    d. bed   e. cradle

6. a. lamp   b. radio   c. sound
    d. light   e. noises

7. a. Glow-worm b. Centipede c. Ladybug
    d. Miss Spider e. Earthworm

104   **3•4**   JAMES AND THE GIANT PEACH

"That crazy Glow-worm has gone to

_____ with her
                    8
light on!"

8. a. bed   b. sleep   c. school

    d. dreamland   e. town

VOCABULARY

**Look at the word in boldface in each exercise that
follows and read carefully the sentence with it. Put an
x in the box before the best meaning or synonym for
the word as it is used in the sentence. Check your
answers using the Answer Key on page 203.**

1. "Lights out," said the Centipede **drowsily**.
   ☐ a. cheerfully
   ☐ b. sleepily
   ☐ c. suddenly

2. . . . the Earthworm was **coiled up** like
   a spring. . . .
   ☐ a. wound up
   ☐ b. walking around
   ☐ c. sleeping sideways

3. . . . James could see her crouching in
   the very center of it, **mumbling** softly
   in her dreams.
   ☐ a. speaking unclearly
   ☐ b. rocking gently
   ☐ c. sleeping soundly

4. . . . James glanced up at the ceiling—
   there he saw a most **extraordinary**
   sight.
   ☐ a. amazing
   ☐ b. uninteresting
   ☐ c. horrible

5. But the Glow-worm didn't **stir**, so the
   Centipede reached out of his hammock
   and picked up one of his boots. . . .
   ☐ a. snore
   ☐ b. sleep
   ☐ c. move

6. "Put out that wretched light!" he shouted,
   hurling the boot up at the ceiling.
   ☐ a. throwing
   ☐ b. removing
   ☐ c. rolling

7. "There is no need to be **rude**," she
   said coldly.
   ☐ a. sick
   ☐ b. unpleasant
   ☐ c. serious

8. Already he was beginning to like his
   new friends very much. They were not
   nearly as **terrible** as they looked.
   ☐ a. awful
   ☐ b. beautiful
   ☐ c. grumpy

Little House in the Big Woods

Laura Ingalls Wilder

Reading Time			Maze
Comprehension			Vocabulary

This passage was taken from *Little House in the Big Woods* by Laura Ingalls Wilder. It is a story about a family that lived in a log cabin many years ago. If you would like to read more of this book, ask for it at your local or school library.

A very long time ago, a little girl lived in the Big Woods of Wisconsin, in a little gray house made of logs.

The great, dark trees of the Big Woods stood all around the house, and beyond them were other trees and beyond them were more trees. As far as a man could go to the north in a day, or a week, or a whole month, there was nothing but woods. There were no houses. There were no roads. There were no people. There were only trees and the wild animals who had their homes among them.

Wolves lived in the Big Woods, and bears, and huge wild cats. Muskrats and mink and otter lived by the streams. Foxes had dens in the hills and deer roamed everywhere.

To the east of the little log house, and to the west, there were miles upon miles of trees, and only a few log houses scattered far apart in the edge of the Big Woods.

So far as the little girl could see, there was only the one little house where she lived with her Father and Mother, her sister Mary, and baby sister Carrie. A wagon track ran before the house, turning and twisting out of sight in the woods where the wild animals lived, but the little girl did not know where it went, nor what might be at the end of it.

The little girl was named Laura and she called her father, Pa, and her mother, Ma. In those days and in that place, children did not say Father and Mother, nor Mamma and Papa, as they do now.

At night, when Laura lay awake in the trundle bed, she listened and could not hear anything at all but the sound of the trees whispering together. Sometimes, far away in the night, a wolf howled. Then he came nearer, and howled again.

It was a scary sound. Laura knew that wolves would eat little girls. But she was safe inside the solid log walls. Her father's gun hung over the door and good old Jack, the brindle bulldog, lay on guard before it. Her father would say,

"Go to sleep, Laura. Jack won't let the wolves in." So Laura snuggled under the covers of the trundle bed, close beside Mary, and went to sleep.

One night her father picked her up out of bed and carried her to the window so that she might see the wolves. There were two of them sitting in front of the house. They looked like shaggy dogs. They pointed their noses at the big, bright moon, and howled.

Jack paced up and down before the door, growling. The hair stood up along his back and he showed his sharp, fierce teeth to the wolves. They howled, but they could not get in.

The house was a comfortable house. Upstairs there was a large attic, pleasant to play in when the rain drummed on the roof.

Read the following questions and statements. For each one, put an *x* in the box before the option that contains the most complete or accurate answer. Check your answers using the Answer Key on page 203.

1. The little log house was surrounded on all sides by
   ☐ a. roads.
   ☐ b. trees.
   ☐ c. people.

2. At night, Laura was frightened by the sound of
   ☐ a. howling wolves.
   ☐ b. barking dogs.
   ☐ c. pouring rain.

3. Jack was
   ☐ a. the family dog.
   ☐ b. Laura's brother.
   ☐ c. a neighbor boy.

4. Which word best describes Laura's home?
   ☐ a. huge
   ☐ b. comfortable
   ☐ c. cold

5. Carrie is
   ☐ a. younger than Laura.
   ☐ b. not afraid of wolves.
   ☐ c. older than Laura.

6. Laura's father made her feel
   ☐ a. taller.
   ☐ b. unhappy.
   ☐ c. safe.

7. How did the howling noises outside affect Jack?
   ☐ a. They frightened him.
   ☐ b. They made him growl.
   ☐ c. They didn't affect him at all.

8. After learning about the wolves, we can guess that
   ☐ a. the Big Woods was a very safe place to play in.
   ☐ b. it was not a good idea to go outside at night alone.
   ☐ c. the Big Woods were probably close to a large town.

The following passage, taken from the selection you have just read, has words omitted from it. Fill in each blank using a word from the set of five words in the column to the right of the passage. Check your answers using the Answer Key on page 203.

A very long time ago, a little girl lived

in the Big Woods of Wisconsin, in a little

gray _____ made of
logs.

The great, dark _____
of the Big Woods stood all around the
house, and beyond them were other trees
and beyond them were more trees. As
far as a man could go to the north
in a day, or a week, or a whole
_____ , there was
nothing but woods. There were no houses.
There were no roads. There were no
people. There were only trees and the
wild animals who had their homes
among them.

Wolves lived in the Big Woods, and
bears, and huge wild cats. Muskrats and
mink and otter lived by the
_____ . Foxes had
dens in the hills and deer roamed
everywhere.

To the east of the little
_____ house, and to
the west, there were miles upon miles of
trees, and only a few log houses
_____ far apart in the
edge of the Big Woods.

So far as the little girl could see, there
was only the one little house where she
lived with her Father and Mother, her
sister Mary, and baby sister Carrie. A
wagon track ran before the house, turning
and twisting out of sight in the woods
where the _____

1. a. home   b. house   c. building
        d. shack   e. cabin

2. a. forest   b. clouds   c. columns
        d. shadows   e. trees

3. a. month   b. age   c. lifetime
        d. season   e. year

4. a. woods   b. streams   c. house
        d. hills   e. dens

5.   a. log   b. brown   c. dark
        d. family   e. tree

6. a. there   b. built   c. scattered
        d. spread   e. located

7. a. forest   b. howling   c. tame
        d. farm   e. wild

animals lived, but the little girl did not know where it went, nor what might be at the _____ of it.
8

8.   a. top   b. edge   c. bottom
         d. end   e. back

VOCABULARY

Look at the word in boldface in each exercise that follows and read carefully the sentence with it. Put an *x* in the box before the best meaning or synonym for the word as it is used in the sentence. Check your answers using the Answer Key on page 203.

1. Foxes had dens in the hills and deer **roamed** everywhere.
   - ☐ a. drank water
   - ☐ b. wandered
   - ☐ c. slept

2. **Muskrats** and mink and otter lived by the streams.
   - ☐ a. kinds of water animals
   - ☐ b. kinds of water plants
   - ☐ c. people who study animals

3. A wagon **track** ran before the house, turning and twisting out of sight. . . .
   - ☐ a. wheel marks
   - ☐ b. sound of wheels
   - ☐ c. pieces of broken wheels

4. . . . good old Jack, the **brindle** bulldog, lay on guard. . . .
   - ☐ a. jumping
   - ☐ b. mean
   - ☐ c. gray and tan

5. Laura **snuggled** under the covers of the trundle bed, close beside Mary, and went to sleep.
   - ☐ a. struggled
   - ☐ b. cuddled
   - ☐ c. shivered

6. They looked like **shaggy** dogs.
   - ☐ a. with low growls
   - ☐ b. with loud howls
   - ☐ c. with thick, rough hair

7. He showed his sharp, **fierce** teeth to the wolves.
   - ☐ a. wild
   - ☐ b. dull
   - ☐ c. friendly

8. Upstairs there was a large attic, warm and pleasant to play in when the rain **drummed** on the roof.
   - ☐ a. beat
   - ☐ b. dripped
   - ☐ c. steamed

Set 4

Racing on the Wind

E. and R. S. Radlauer

Reading Time			Maze
Comprehension			Vocabulary

The following passage was taken from *Racing on the Wind* by E. and R. S. Radlauer. It is a book about the sports of flying and sailing done in different vehicles. If you would like to read more, ask for the book at either your school or neighborhood library.

When the wind blows, many things go. The things and the people in them may go up, down, around, or whatever way the wind goes. They may go over water, on the water, over land, or on land. History is filled with stories of people who used wind and air for fun and travel. One story that goes back about 3,000 years into history tells of two Greek men who escaped from prison by using wings made of feathers and wax. The story says the wax wings melted when one man flew too near the sun. His feathers fell off and he crashed into the sea. If those Greeks had used *hang glide* or *self-soaring* wings for their prison escape, there wouldn't have been any wax for the sun to melt. Of course, no one believes they got near the sun, anyway.

For self-soaring or hang gliding there should be wind, plenty of it. A wind of 20 miles per hour or more is good for flying. Before flying, a rider sets up his kite at the top of a hill. The kite must be unfolded and set up facing into the wind. If the front or point isn't facing the wind, the kite may go flying without the rider.

Hang glide kites are made of tightly woven cloth, lightweight metal rods, and strong wires. The cloth is so tightly woven that it's almost *airtight*. The rods and wires should be made of very strong material. If something should break during a flight—well, remember the Greeks.

People have always wanted to fly, and people have always wanted to add beauty to their lives. Beauty can come from colors, shapes, and forms. Self-soaring people add beauty to their kites with colors and decorations. Quite often a person may have a kite custom-made by a professional kite builder. The kite builder can let the buyer pick the cloth for color and decoration. But when it comes to the shape, the professional builder doesn't let the buyer have much say. A kite has to be built to fly. That's why the shape is important. People who build their own kites can decorate them anyway they like, but if the shape isn't right, they wouldn't do much flying.

After being strapped in, a hang glide kite flier is ready to go. The flight starts with a downhill run into the wind. The wind catches the kite and gives the rider the lift needed to fly. For the first part of the ride, the rider tries for speed and altitude. Without these, a flight may be over before it even starts. As soon as the kite gains speed and altitude, a flier can start to control the direction of flight. For a right turn, the rider leans to the right and moves the steering bar to the left. This tips the kite to the right and it makes a turn. For a left turn, the rider leans left.

COMPREHENSION

Read the following questions and statements. For each one, put an _x_ in the box before the option that contains the most complete or accurate answer. Check your answers using the Answer Key on page 204.

1. How strong a wind is needed for good hang gliding?
   - ☐ a. 10 miles per hour or more
   - ☐ b. 20 miles per hour or more
   - ☐ c. 55 miles per hour or more

2. A rider should set up a kite
   - ☐ a. at the top of a hill.
   - ☐ b. on an airport runway.
   - ☐ c. on a mountain top.

3. Who decides on the shape of a kite?
   - ☐ a. the buyer
   - ☐ b. the kite builder
   - ☐ c. the government

4. After being strapped in, one begins the flight by
   - ☐ a. moving the steering bar to the left.
   - ☐ b. running downhill into the wind.
   - ☐ c. calling the airport control tower.

5. The fact that history is filled with stories of how people used air for travel shows that
   - ☐ a. people have never wanted to fly until the 20th century.
   - ☐ b. people have always been interested in flying.
   - ☐ c. people have never even thought about flying until recently.

6. Which of the following seems to be most important in building a hang glide kite?
   - ☐ a. the color of the kite
   - ☐ b. the kind of material used
   - ☐ c. the shape of the kite

7. To have a successful flight, a person needs
   - ☐ a. a crash helmet.
   - ☐ b. plenty of wind.
   - ☐ c. plenty of wax.

8. When the kite begins traveling high enough and fast enough, the hang glide flier should
   - ☐ a. end the flight right away.
   - ☐ b. jump to the ground.
   - ☐ c. control the direction of the flight.

MAZE

The following passage, taken from the selection you have just read, has words omitted from it. Fill in each blank using a word from the set of five words in the column to the right of the passage. Check your answers using the Answer Key on page 204.

Hang glide kites are made of tightly woven cloth, lightweight metal rods, and strong wires. The _____ is so tightly woven that it's almost *airtight*. The rods and _____ should be made of very strong material. If something should break during a _____—well, remember the Greeks.

People have always wanted to _____ , and people have always wanted to add beauty to their lives. Beauty can come from colors, shapes, and forms. Self-soaring people add _____ to their kites with colors and decorations. Quite often a person may have a kite custom-made by a _____ kite builder. The kite builder can let the buyer pick the cloth for color and decoration. But when it comes to the _____ , the professional builder doesn't let the buyer have much say. A kite has to be built to fly. That's why the shape is

1. a. wires   b. material   c. rods   d. kite   e. cloth

2. a. metal   b. wires   c. straps   d. bar   e. kites

3. a. ride   b. lift-off   c. glide   d. flight   e. trip

4. a. color   b. soar   c. glide   d. build   e. fly

5. a. beauty   b. speed   c. adventure   d. detail   e. form

6. a. true   b. special   c. expert   d. professional   e. Greek

7. a. shape   b. decoration   c. cloth   d. flight   e. color

_____ . People who
build their own kites can decorate them
anyway they like, but if the shape isn't
right, they wouldn't do much flying.

8. a. important   b. needed   c. square

   d. built   e. correct

**Look at the word in boldface in each exercise that
follows and read carefully the sentence with it. Put an
x in the box before the best meaning or synonym for
the word as it is used in the sentence. Check your
answers using the Answer Key on page 204.**

1. For **self-soaring** or hang gliding
   there should be wind, plenty
   of it.
   - ☐ a. a way of flying without power
   - ☐ b. something out of the ordinary
   - ☐ c. facing into the wind

2. A wind of 20 miles **per** hour is good
   for flying.
   - ☐ a. for every
   - ☐ b. through
   - ☐ c. by

3. Hang glide kites are made of tightly
   woven cloth, lightweight metal rods,
   and strong wires.
   - ☐ a. stretched on all sides
   - ☐ b. shaped into a triangle
   - ☐ c. made by weaving

4. The cloth is so tightly woven that it's
   almost **airtight**.
   - ☐ a. waterproof
   - ☐ b. without holes
   - ☐ c. lightweight

5. . . . a person may have a kite **custom-
   made** by a professional kite builder.
   - ☐ a. test-flown
   - ☐ b. specially made
   - ☐ c. decorated by hand

6. But when it comes to the shape, the
   professional builder doesn't let the
   buyer have much say.
   - ☐ a. a person who is learning a skill
   - ☐ b. a person who earns a living
   - ☐ c. a person who has a hobby

7. For the first part of the ride, the rider
   tries for speed and **altitude**.
   - ☐ a. strength
   - ☐ b. distance
   - ☐ c. height

8. As soon as the kite gains speed and
   altitude, a flier can **control** the
   direction of flight.
   - ☐ a. guide
   - ☐ b. stop
   - ☐ c. push

Henry Reed's Journey

Keith Robertson

Reading Time ☐   ☐ Maze

Comprehension ☐   ☐ Vocabulary

The following passage, from *Henry Reed's Journey* by Keith Robertson, is the story of a boy taking his first trip across America. If you are interested in reading more of this book, ask for it at your school or public library.

My name is Henry Harris Reed and this is my journal. It is my private property and in case it gets lost, please return it to me in care of my uncle, Mr. J. Alfred Harris, RD 1, Grover's Corner, Princeton, N.J. I'll send you whatever you spend in postage. It's important that I get it back as I am going to make it into a book and publish it.

I guess I'd better explain how I happen to be flying to San Francisco. My father is in the diplomatic service. Last summer we were living in Naples, and I flew to the United States and spent the summer with my Uncle Al and Aunt Mabel in Grover's Corner, New Jersey. I had a lot of fun, and I guess my aunt and uncle didn't mind having me too much, because they invited me back again this summer. This time, however, I am not crossing the Atlantic Ocean. About six months ago my father was transferred to Manila, and so I am flying across the Pacific and will arrive in San Francisco.

Last year I kept a journal of what I did and used it as a report when school opened. I got an "A" on it. Miss Prescott, my English teacher, said it was very good, although she did complain about the pages being sort of grimy. She says anyone who keeps a journal should always wash his hands before writing in it just as he should before meals. That's silly. Can you

imagine Robinson Crusoe going down to the stream and washing his hands every time he wrote in his journal? He would have been caught by the cannibals long before he finished his book. Probably what upset Miss Prescott was the angleworm that got pressed between pages 42 and 43. I remember using a worm as a marker, but I wouldn't have closed the notebook on it. I wonder if Midge could have done that? That's the sort of trick she'd think was hilarious.

Midge Glass was my partner in a research business in Grover's Corner last summer. She was the only person under forty living there, so I didn't have much choice. She turned out to be a good sport and very smart, even if she is a girl. We got to be very good friends. Midge doesn't giggle, and giggling is the main thing wrong with most girls.

Mr. Glass is a research chemist, and he is attending a convention in San Francisco. Midge and Mrs. Glass are with him, and they are all going to drive back to New Jersey. The trip is their vacation. Since I was due to arrive in San Francisco at the same time they planned to be there, I was invited to drive back with them. That was a lucky break for me, and I am looking forward to the trip. I've been all over Europe and part of Asia, but I haven't seen much of the United States.

Read the following questions and statements. For each one, put an *x* in the box before the option that contains the most complete or accurate answer. Check your answers using the Answer Key on page 204.

1. If his journal gets lost, Henry would like it to be returned to
   ☐ a. Rhode Island.
   ☐ b. New Jersey.
   ☐ c. San Francisco.

2. While he is writing this journal entry Henry is
   ☐ a. on a diplomatic mission.
   ☐ b. flying to San Francisco.
   ☐ c. crossing the Atlantic Ocean.

3. Last summer Henry visited
   ☐ a. Grover's Corner.
   ☐ b. Manila.
   ☐ c. Naples.

4. Henry's English teacher is
   ☐ a. Mr. Glass.
   ☐ b. Mr. J. Alfred Harris.
   ☐ c. Miss Prescott.

5. Henry's father
   ☐ a. moves frequently.
   ☐ b. has lived in Manila for two years.
   ☐ c. is going back to Naples.

6. Henry considers washing his hands before journal writing silly because
   ☐ a. water is scarce in Naples.
   ☐ b. journal entries aren't always planned.
   ☐ c. the pages will stick together.

7. Grover's Corner
   ☐ a. has few children.
   ☐ b. attracts many tourists.
   ☐ c. is close to San Francisco.

8. Henry is glad to be traveling in the Glass's car because he will
   ☐ a. visit the Atlantic Ocean again.
   ☐ b. see some of the United States.
   ☐ c. enjoy Mr. Glass's conversation.

MAZE

The following passage, taken from the selection you have just read, has words omitted from it. Fill in each blank using a word from the set of five words in the column to the right of the passage. Check your answers using the Answer Key on page 204.

My name is Henry Harris Reed and this is my journal. It is my private _____ and in case it

1. a. life   b. thoughts   c. property
   d. ideas   e. entrance

gets lost, please _____

_____ it to me in care of my uncle, Mr. J. Alfred
2

Harris, RD 1, Grover's Corner, Princeton,

N.J. I'll send you whatever you spend in

postage. It's important that I get it

_____ as I am going
3

to make it into a book and publish it.

I guess I'd better _____
4

how I happen to be flying to San

Francisco. My father is in the diplomatic

service. Last summer we were living in

Naples, and I flew to the United States

and spent the _____
5

with my Uncle Al and Aunt Mabel in

Grover's Corner, New Jersey. I had a lot

of fun, and I guess my aunt and uncle

didn't mind having me too much, because

they invited me _____
6

again this summer. This time, however, I

am not crossing the Atlantic Ocean.

About six _____ ago
7

my father was transferred to Manila,

and so I am flying across the Pacific and

will _____ in
8

San Francisco.

2.   a. leave   b. return   c. give

d. send   e. mail

3.   a. read   b. sent   c. back

d. lost   e. written

4. a. ask   b. explain   c. wonder

d. think   e. answer

5.   a. time   b. summer   c. weeks

d. vacation   e. holiday

6. a. back   b. quickly   c. alone

d. for   e. happily

7. a. hours   b. months   c. weeks

d. years   e. times

8.   a. live   b. vacation   c. travel

d. arrive   e. sightsee

VOCABULARY

**Look at the word in boldface in each exercise that
follows and read carefully the sentence with it. Put an
x in the box before the best meaning or synonym for
the word as it is used in the sentence. Check your
answers using the Answer Key on page 204.**

1. It is my **private** property and
   in case it gets lost, please return
   it to me.
   - ☐ a. legal
   - ☐ b. borrowed
   - ☐ c. personal

2. I'm going to make it into a book and
   publish it.
   - ☐ a. print
   - ☐ b. sign
   - ☐ c. read

3. I guess I'd better **explain**
   how I happen to be flying to
   San Francisco.
   - ☐ a. ask
   - ☐ b. tell
   - ☐ c. wonder

4. About six months ago my
   father was **transferred** to
   Manila, and so I am flying
   across the Pacific and will
   arrive in San Francisco.
   - ☐ a. introduced
   - ☐ b. moved
   - ☐ c. visited

5. . . . she did complain about the pages
   being sort of **grimy**. She says that
   anyone who keeps a journal should
   always wash his hands before writing
   in it. . . .
   - ☐ a. complicated
   - ☐ b. rude
   - ☐ c. dirty

6. That's the sort of trick she'd think
   was **hilarious**.
   - ☐ a. sincere
   - ☐ b. sad
   - ☐ c. funny

7. Midge Glass was my **partner** in a
   research business in Grover's Corner
   last summer.
   - ☐ a. coworker
   - ☐ b. enemy
   - ☐ c. boss

8. . . . I was **due** to arrive in San
   Francisco at the same time they
   planned to be there. . . .
   - ☐ a. about
   - ☐ b. expected
   - ☐ c. delayed

Behind the Scenes
of a Broadway Musical

Bill Powers

Reading Time [   ]   [   ] Maze

Comprehension [   ]   [   ] Vocabulary

Behind the Scenes of a Broadway Musical by Bill Powers talks about what really goes on backstage before a big Broadway show takes place. If you are interested in reading more of this book, ask for it at your school or local library.

The entire cast of *Really Rosie* was made up of very young actors. Most of them could not read music. They had to learn the songs by ear. To speed up the process, musical director Joel Silberman used the following technique during the first week of rehearsals to help Wade Raley learn his long solo in "One Was Johnny."

Joel sang while Wade listened and followed the lyrics in his script. Then Wade sang with Joel guiding him through the song. Next, Joel sang a short selection and Wade repeated it. They went through the entire song this way. Then Joel made a tape of Wade singing so Wade could take it home and study it.

A few days later, when Wade was sure of the lyrics, another tape was made. This time Wade and Joel sang together. The purpose of the new tape was to help Wade hit the proper notes. This method was used only for the solos. When the entire cast sang, Joel had to teach them their parts during rehearsal, which meant a lot of time at the piano.

The music for the play was written for the piano. Music for the other instruments had to be written also. Most composers do not have the necessary skills for this. The task of expanding the score is usually assigned to a musical arranger.

For *Really Rosie*, Joel Silberman did the arrangements. After teaching the cast the songs, he was ready to begin working on the arrangements. First he had to see how Pat Birch was going to stage each musical number. While Pat Birch was staging the songs, Joel began making notes in his score to indicate how and where he wanted the other instruments to play. If the song was a solo, the band had to play softly enough so the singer could be heard. But if it was sung by a chorus, the whole band could be used and the sound could be much fuller. Joel could not work on the arrangements until the songs were staged. When he did start he had to work furiously to get them finished on time.

When all the parts for all the instruments were written, they were turned over to a copyist. The copyist would copy the music for each instrument by hand on separate musical sheets so that every musician would have a score.

Really Rosie used a small backstage band of five musicians, including Joel, who conducted from the piano. The five musicians played a total of nine instruments. Even for this small group, the job done by Joel's assistant, Alex Rybeck, and copyist Meredith Marcellus, was a huge one. There were eleven musical numbers for the nine instruments, which meant that nearly one hundred parts had to be copied.

Using the songs in the show, Joel also had to compose an overture. This is the music played just before the curtain rises and the show begins. The overture is meant to reflect the spirit of the play. It should put the audience in the right mood. Joel worked hard to create an exciting one. Just after he finished writing it, he described it to Alex one day during a lunch break. Joel was happy with what he had written and Alex applauded.

COMPREHENSION

Read the following questions and statements. For each one, put an *x* in the box before the option that contains the most complete or accurate answer. Check your answers using the Answer Key on page 204.

1. The young actors in *Really Rosie*
   - ☐ a. could read music.
   - ☐ b. needed shorter rehearsals.
   - ☐ c. had to learn the songs by ear.

2. The taped song helped Wade to
   - ☐ a. speak more clearly.
   - ☐ b. remember to go to rehearsals.
   - ☐ c. learn to sing his solo.

3. *Really Rosie*'s musical director was
   - ☐ a. Joel Silberman.
   - ☐ b. Pat Birch.
   - ☐ c. Wade Riley.

4. How many instruments were in the band?
   - ☐ a. nine
   - ☐ b. five
   - ☐ c. eleven

5. While he was arranging the score, Joel had
   - ☐ a. no help from anyone.
   - ☐ b. help from two people.
   - ☐ c. to fire several people.

6. Without separate scores the musicians would
   - ☐ a. have needed to play more instruments.
   - ☐ b. have needed to play more numbers.
   - ☐ c. not have known what music to play.

7. If there are nine instruments and five musicians,
   - ☐ a. the music will be very soft.
   - ☐ b. some of the musicians must play more than one instrument.
   - ☐ c. the musicians will need to rehearse longer.

8. During the show's performance, you will hear the overture at
   - ☐ a. intermission.
   - ☐ b. the beginning.
   - ☐ c. the end.

MAZE

The following passage, taken from the selection you have just read, has words omitted from it. Fill in each blank using a word from the set of five words in the column to the right of the passage. Check your answers using the Answer Key on page 204.

The entire cast of *Really Rosie* was made up of very young actors. Most of them could not read _____ . They had to learn the songs by ear. To speed up the process, musical director Joel Silberman used the following technique during the first week of _____ to help Wade Raley learn his long solo in "One Was Johnny."

Joel sang while Wade _____ and followed the lyrics in his script. Then Wade sang with Joel guiding him through the _____ . Next, Joel sang a short selection and Wade repeated it. They went through the entire song this way. Then Joel made a _____ of Wade singing so Wade could take it home and study it.

A few days later, when Wade was sure of the _____ , another tape was made. This time Wade and Joel sang together. The _____ of the new tape was to help Wade hit the proper notes. This method was used only for the solos.

1. a. lyrics   b. songs   c. newspaper
    d. books   e. music

2. a. work   b. practice   c. rehearsals
    d. singing   e. learning

3. a. played   b. listened   c. worked
    d. danced   e. sang

4. a. music   b. song   c. lyrics
    d. play   e. steps

5. a. tape   b. record   c. photograph
    d. painting   e. book

6. a. play   b. lyrics   c. music
    d. song   e. part

7. a. color   b. reason   c. recording
    d. function   e. purpose

When the _____ cast
sang, Joel had to teach them their parts
during rehearsal, which meant a lot of
time at the piano.

8. a. younger   b. real   c. entire

   d. musical   e. children's

VOCABULARY

**Look at the word in boldface in each exercise that
follows and read carefully the sentence with it. Put an
x in the box before the best meaning or synonym for
the word as it is used in the sentence. Check your
answers using the Answer Key on page 204.**

1. The entire **cast** of *Really Rosie* was
   made up of very young actors.
   ☐ a. directors
   ☐ b. performers
   ☐ c. audience

2. To speed up the process, musical
   director Joel Silberman used the
   following **technique** during the first
   week of rehearsals. . . .
   ☐ a. method
   ☐ b. musical style
   ☐ c. schedule

3. Joel sang while Wade listened and
   followed the **lyrics** in his script.
   ☐ a. directions
   ☐ b. speeches
   ☐ c. words of a song

4. When the entire cast sang, Joel had to
   teach them their parts during **rehearsal**.
   ☐ a. practice session
   ☐ b. recess
   ☐ c. performance

5. Most composers do not have the
   necessary skills for this.
   ☐ a. writing
   ☐ b. basic
   ☐ c. needed

6. If the song was a **solo**, the band had to
   play softly enough so the singer could
   be heard.
   ☐ a. performed by many singers
   ☐ b. performed by one person
   ☐ c. performed by the band

7. When he did start he had to work
   furiously to get them finished on time.
   ☐ a. very hard
   ☐ b. occasionally
   ☐ c. for an hour

8. Using the songs in the show, Joel had
   to **compose** an overture.
   ☐ a. sing
   ☐ b. write
   ☐ c. direct

The Good-Guy Cake

Barbara Dillon

Reading Time			Maze
Comprehension			Vocabulary

This passge is from *The Good-Guy Cake* by
Barbara Dillon. The book describes the problems
a boy has as the youngest member of his family.
If you are interested in reading more of this
book, ask for it at your school or public library.

Martin Bennett, get out of my closet this instant!" yelled Martin's sister, Mary. "What are you doing in this room anyway?"

"I'm looking for my ball," explained Martin, backing hastily toward the door.

"Well, it's not in here," Mary said. She looked at her brother more closely. "What have you got all over your mouth?" she demanded.

"Nothing," said Martin, nervously putting his sticky hands behind his back.

"It's chocolate!" Mary screamed. "You found that Mars Bar in my sewing box. You stole my candy!"

Martin didn't stop to answer. He turned and ran.

"If I ever find you in here again, I'll kill you!" Mary shouted after him.

Martin bounded downstairs just as fast as his legs could carry him.

"Martin, look what you're doing to my new wallpaper!" cried his mother. She was standing in the hallway glaring up at him. Martin glanced in alarm at the wall next to him. It was covered with chocolatey finger marks.

Oh-oh, I'm in trouble, he thought.

"How many times have I told you to keep your hands off the wall and use the banister?" his mother wailed. "That's what it's there for."

"I'm sorry," said Martin. "I'll remember next time."

He particularly wanted his mother to be in a good mood today, because he had something very important to ask her, something he and his best friend, Charlie Miles, had just finished talking about on the telephone. As a matter of fact, he had been on his way downstairs to find her when he had been sidetracked by the interesting possibilities of Mary's empty room. Now he would have to wait awhile until his mother cooled off.

Martin went into the living room and snapped on the television. He snapped it off again, got down on his hands and knees to look for a quarter that he had lost under the couch the week before, and then, figuring he had given his mother enough time to recover, headed doggedly for the kitchen.

Mrs. Bennett was busy swabbing the floor with her sponge mop.

"Don't come in," she said sharply. "The floor is all wet."

"Can-I-go-to-the-school-fair-next-week-on-my-bike-Charlie-Miles'-mom-is-letting-him-and-I-would-be-very-careful-and-ride-over-to-the-side-of-the-road-so-I-don't-get-killed." Martin took a deep breath and looked eagerly at his mother.

"You would have to go along the Post

Road to get to the school," Mrs. Bennett said, without looking up from her mopping. "There would be too much traffic. I would worry the whole time you were gone."

"Charlie Miles' mom isn't going to worry," said Martin. "And I'm a better rider than Charlie is."

"Well, I can't help it. I would worry," said his mother, squeezing out the mop into the bucket at her side.

"I would go really slowly and not try anything crazy," Martin promised.

"No," said his mother firmly.

COMPREHENSION

Read the following questions and statements. For each one, put an *x* in the box before the option that contains the most complete or accurate answer. Check your answers using the Answer Key on page 204.

1. Martin was caught
   - ☐ a. riding his bike to the school fair.
   - ☐ b. watching television.
   - ☐ c. eating his sister's chocolate.

2. Mrs. Bennett
   - ☐ a. wanted Martin to use the banister.
   - ☐ b. had just finished washing the floor.
   - ☐ c. was cooling off by the fan.

3. Martin hoped that his mother was in a good mood because
   - ☐ a. his sister was mad at him.
   - ☐ b. he had something important to ask her.
   - ☐ c. he had to telephone Charlie.

4. Martin looked for the lost quarter
   - ☐ a. in Mary's closet.
   - ☐ b. behind the television.
   - ☐ c. under the couch.

5. Martin
   - ☐ a. lied to his sister.
   - ☐ b. lost his ball in Mary's room.
   - ☐ c. gave his sister a candy bar.

6. Martin makes Mary
   - ☐ a. happy.
   - ☐ b. angry.
   - ☐ c. giggle.

7. The Post Road is a
   - ☐ a. quiet street.
   - ☐ b. dead end.
   - ☐ c. busy road.

8. Martin's mother
   - ☐ a. is concerned about her son.
   - ☐ b. doesn't care if he goes to the fair.
   - ☐ c. is sure that Martin will be perfectly safe.

MAZE

The following passage, taken from the selection you have just read, has words omitted from it. Fill in each blank using a word from the set of five words in the column to the right of the passage. Check your answers using the Answer Key on page 204.

"Martin Bennett, get out of my closet this instant!" yelled Martin's

_____ , Mary.

"What are you doing in this

_____ anyway?"

"I'm looking for my ball," explained Martin, backing hastily toward the

_____ .

"Well, it's not in here," Mary said. She looked at her brother more closely. "What have you got all over your

_____ ?" she demanded.

"Nothing," said Martin, nervously putting his sticky

_____ behind his back.

"It's chocolate!" Mary screamed. "You found that Mars Bar in my sewing box. You stole my _____ !"

Martin didn't stop to answer. He turned and _____ . . . .

Martin bounded downstairs just as fast as his _____ could carry him.

1. a. friend   b. mother   c. cousin
     d. sister   e. aunt

2. a. house   b. area   c. room
     d. trouble   e. place

3. a. door   b. kitchen   c. stairs
     d. closet   e. exit

4. a. tongue   b. face   c. teeth
     d. mouth   e. shirt

5. a. nose   b. face   c. foot
     d. hands   e. mouth

6. a. fortune   b. candy   c. bar
     d. money   e. treasure

7. a. ran   b. screamed   c. fell
     d. jumped   e. walked

8. a. friend   b. body   c. legs
     d. mind   e. feet

Look at the word in boldface in each exercise that follows and read carefully the sentence with it. Put an *x* in the box before the best meaning or synonym for the word as it is used in the sentence. Check your answers using the Answer Key on page 204.

1. "I'm looking for my ball," explained Martin, backing **hastily** toward the door.
   - ☐ a. clumsily
   - ☐ b. quickly
   - ☐ c. steadily

2. Martin **bounded** downstairs just as fast as his legs could carry him.
   - ☐ a. walked
   - ☐ b. fell
   - ☐ c. jumped

3. She was standing in the hallway **glaring** up at him.
   - ☐ a. staring angrily
   - ☐ b. winking slyly
   - ☐ c. smiling sweetly

4. Martin glanced in **alarm** at the wall next to him. It was covered with chocolatey finger marks.
   - ☐ a. excitement
   - ☐ b. fear
   - ☐ c. giggles

5. . . . he had been on his way downstairs when he had been **sidetracked** by the interesting possibilities of Mary's empty room.
   - ☐ a. distracted
   - ☐ b. silenced
   - ☐ c. attacked

6. . . . then, figuring he had given his mother enough time to recover, headed **doggedly** for the kitchen.
   - ☐ a. stubbornly
   - ☐ b. shyly
   - ☐ c. loudly

7. Mrs. Bennett was busy **swabbing** the floor with her sponge mop.
   - ☐ a. brushing
   - ☐ b. washing
   - ☐ c. painting

8. "No," said his mother **firmly**.
   - ☐ a. sternly
   - ☐ b. suddenly
   - ☐ c. quietly

Gravity

Vicki Cobb and Kathy Darling

Reading Time [ ]   [ ] Maze

Comprehension [ ]   [ ] Vocabulary

This passage is from *Bet You Can't!* by Vicki Cobb and Kathy Darling. The book is full of scientific tricks and impossibilities that you *won't* be able to try out. If you are interested in reading more of this book, ask for it at your school or public library.

Gravity is the biggest downer of all time. True? Yes. But, surprise! Gravity can pull sideways or even up. The sun is pulling on the Earth in a direction that is anything but down.

Gravity is the force of attraction between two masses. When it's the only force operating, it draws the smaller mass to the larger one. The reason we think of gravity as a downer is because the most familiar example is the force of attraction between the giant Earth and our body.

One way gravity exerts its force is very curious. All the weight of a body seems to be concentrated at a single center point. If a body has a supporting base, its "center of gravity" must be located directly over the base or the body will tip over. When an object has a regular shape, like the earth, it is easy to locate the center of gravity because it is at the geometric center. A seesaw is balanced at its geometric center, its center of gravity.

Irregularly shaped objects, like the human body, do not have a center of gravity that necessarily coincides with the geometric center. In fact, the center of gravity can be moved around. The artful use of gravity can throw you totally off balance. Wanna bet?

BET YOU CAN'T PICK UP A DOLLAR BILL THAT'S RIGHT IN FRONT OF YOU!

THE SETUP: Stand with your heels against a wall and your feet together. Place a dollar bill on the floor about a foot in front of your feet. Try to pick up the dollar without moving your feet or bending your knees.

THE FIX: That dollar is as safe as if it were in the bank. You can't pick it up. Here's why. When you stand straight against the wall, your center of gravity is over your feet (base) as it should be. When you bend forward, you move your center of gravity forward. In order to keep your balance, you must move your feet forward too. This maintains the base under the center of gravity needed for stability. Since the rules of this trick don't allow you to move your feet, you're dollarless. And if you persist in trying to pick it up, you'll fall flat on your face!

BET YOU CAN'T JUMP!

THE SETUP: Keep your heels, hips, and shoulders against the wall. Without leaning forward, try to jump. What's the matter? Are your feet stuck to the floor?

BET YOU CAN'T LIFT YOUR FOOT OFF THE FLOOR!

THE SETUP: Turn your right side to the wall. Put your right foot and cheek against the wall. Now try to lift your left foot off the floor.

THE FIX: Both of these stunts require you to shift your center of gravity away from the support base. The first can't be done without falling over, and the second can't be done without moving the wall. The body maintains balance with little adjustments so automatic that we never think about them.

COMPREHENSION

Read the following questions and statements. For each one, put an *x* in the box before the option that contains the most complete or accurate answer. Check your answers using the Answer Key on page 204.

1. Gravity
   - ☐ a. cannot pull you up.
   - ☐ b. is the force of attraction between two masses.
   - ☐ c. cannot exert its force on human beings.

2. When gravity is the only force operating, it
   - ☐ a. cannot control irregularly shaped objects.
   - ☐ b. changes the Earth's geometric center.
   - ☐ c. draws the smaller mass to the larger one.

3. The "dollar bill on the floor" trick shows how
   - ☐ a. the center of gravity affects stability.
   - ☐ b. you can defy gravity.
   - ☐ c. gravity changes your flexibility.

4. "Bet you can't lift your foot off the floor" can only be done by
   - ☐ a. moving the wall.
   - ☐ b. falling over.
   - ☐ c. bending your knees.

5. This selection proves that
   - ☐ a. betting can help you control gravity.
   - ☐ b. gravity draws a large mass to a smaller one.
   - ☐ c. your body automatically makes adjustments to maintain balance.

6. When the authors say that your dollar is "as safe as if it were in the bank," they mean that
   - ☐ a. most thieves don't understand the force of gravity.
   - ☐ b. following all the rules of the stunt makes it impossible to remove the money.
   - ☐ c. gravity is holding the dollar bill to the floor.

7. These stunts would be easy if
 □ a. we could adjust our geometric centers.
 □ b. the scientific principles were changed.
 □ c. gravity did not exist.

8. The principle of gravity
 □ a. can be shown by physically changing the center of gravity.
 □ b. is best explained by scientific articles.
 □ c. always involves several research scientists.

MAZE

The following passage, taken from the selection you have just read, has words omitted from it. Fill in each blank using a word from the set of five words in the column to the right of the passage. Check your answers using the Answer Key on page 204.

Gravity is the biggest downer of all time. True? Yes. But, surprise! _____ can pull sideways or even up. The sun is pulling on the Earth in a direction that is anything but _____ .

Gravity is the force of attraction between two masses. When it's the only _____ operating, it draws the smaller mass to the larger one. The _____ we think of gravity as a downer is because the most familiar example is the force of attraction between the giant Earth and our _____ .

One way gravity exerts its force is very curious. All the weight of a body seems to be concentrated at a single center point. If a body has a supporting base, its "center

1. a. You   b. Gravity   c. Force
   d. Earth   e. It

2. a. up   b. sideways   c. frontward
   d. down   e. backward

3. a. means   b. kind   c. direction
   d. basis   e. force

4. a. purpose   b. ability   c. reason
   d. thought   e. idea

5. a. sun   b. system   c. world
   d. planet   e. body

of gravity" must be located directly over the base or the body will tip over. When an object has a regular shape, like the Earth, it is easy to locate the center of gravity because it is at the

_____ center. A
        6
seesaw is balanced at its geometric center, its center of gravity.

_____ shaped
        7
objects, like the human body, do not have a center of gravity that necessarily coincides with the geometric center. In fact, the _____ of
                                    8
gravity can be moved around. The artful use of gravity can throw you totally off balance.

6. a. weighted   b. true   c. geometric

   d. basic   e. gravity

7. a. Large b. Regularly c. Irregularly

   d. Small e. Circular

8. a. center   b. force   c. power

   d. strength   e. pull

VOCABULARY

Look at the word in boldface in each exercise that follows and read carefully the sentence with it. Put an *x* in the box before the best meaning or synonym for the word as it is used in the sentence. Check your answers using the Answer Key on page 204.

1. The reason we think of gravity as a downer is because the most **familiar** example is the force of attraction between the giant Earth and our body.
   ☐ a. common
   ☐ b. scientific
   ☐ c. misunderstood

2. One way gravity exerts its **force** is very curious.
   ☐ a. end
   ☐ b. base
   ☐ c. strength

3. All the weight of a body seems to be **concentrated** at a single point.
   - ☐ a. spread
   - ☐ b. focused
   - ☐ c. crushed

4. **Irregularly** shaped objects like the human body do not have a center of gravity that necessarily coincides with the geometric center.
   - ☐ a. smoothly
   - ☐ b. mechanically
   - ☐ c. unevenly

5. In fact, the center of gravity can be moved around. The **artful** use of gravity can throw you totally off balance.
   - ☐ a. clever
   - ☐ b. balanced
   - ☐ c. falling

6. This maintains the base under the center of gravity needed for **stability**.
   - ☐ a. motion
   - ☐ b. steadiness
   - ☐ c. rhythm

7. Both of these **stunts** require you to shift your center of gravity away from the support base.
   - ☐ a. activities
   - ☐ b. materials
   - ☐ c. tricks

8. The body maintains balance with little **adjustments** so automatic we never think about them.
   - ☐ a. changes
   - ☐ b. plots
   - ☐ c. attentions

Set 5

The Enormous Egg

Oliver Butterworth

Reading Time | | | Maze

Comprehension | | | Vocabulary

This passage was taken from *The Enormous Egg* by Oliver Butterworth. It is a story about what happened when a chick laid a huge egg and hatched a dinosaur. If you enjoyed this passage and would like to read more, ask for the book at either your school or neighborhood library.

Dr. Ziemer arrived while we were still staring at the thing in the nest. He jumped out of his car and came running out to us in the backyard. He was wearing a red bathrobe over his pajamas, and he looked pretty excited.

He ran up to the nest and looked in. His eyes opened up wide and he knelt down on the ground and stared and stared and stared. After a long while he said softly, "That's it. By George, that's just what it is." Then he stared for another long time and finally he shook his head and said, "It can't be true, but there it is."

He got up off his knees and looked around at us. His eyes were just sparkling, he was so excited. He put his hand on my shoulder, and I could feel he was quivering. "An amazing thing's happened," he said, in a kind of whisper. "I don't know how to account for it. It must be some sort of freak biological mixup that might happen once in a thousand years."

"But what is it?" I asked.

Dr. Ziemer turned and pointed a trembling finger at the nest. "Believe it or not, you people have hatched out a *dinosaur.*"

We just looked at him.

"Sound incredible, I know," he said, "and I can't explain it, but there it is. I've

seen too many Triceratops skulls to be mistaken about this one."

"But—but how could it be a dinosaur?" Pop asked.

"Goodness gracious!" Mom spluttered. "And right here in our backyard. It doesn't seem hardly right. And on a Sunday, too."

Cynthia was pretty interested by now, and kept peeking into the nest and making faces, the way she did when Pop brought a bowl of frogs' legs into the kitchen one time. I guess girls just naturally don't like crawly things too much. To tell the truth, I don't either sometimes, but this thing that had just hatched out looked kind of cute to me. Maybe that was because I had taken care of the egg so long. I felt as if the little dinosaur was almost one of the family.

We stood around for a long while looking at the strange new thing on the nest, trying to let the idea soak in that we had a dinosaur. After Dr. Ziemer calmed down a little, he and Pop tightened up the chicken wire to make sure the little animal wasn't going to crawl out. Dr. Ziemer watched the poor old hen for a time, and then he wondered if perhaps she ought not to be taken out before she went out of her mind. Pop figured that it might be a good idea and he picked her up and put her outside the pen. She acted a little dazed at first, but pretty soon she followed the other hens and began scratching for worms like the rest of them.

"I've never seen such a surprised hen in my life," Dr. Ziemer said.

COMPREHENSION

Read the following questions and statements. For each one, put an *x* in the box before the option that contains the most complete or accurate answer. Check your answers using the Answer Key on page 205.

1. What did Dr. Ziemer find in the nest?
   - ☐ a. a chick
   - ☐ b. a dinosaur
   - ☐ c. a rooster

2. Dr. Ziemer was very
   - ☐ a. excited.
   - ☐ b. disappointed.
   - ☐ c. terrified.

3. The action in this story takes place
   - ☐ a. in a backyard.
   - ☐ b. at an animal hospital.
   - ☐ c. at the zoo.

4. The hen appeared to be
   - ☐ a. unhappy.
   - ☐ b. sick.
   - ☐ c. dazed.

5. *The Enormous Egg* is a
   - ☐ a. sad story.
   - ☐ b. serious story.
   - ☐ c. funny story.

6. When the family finds out what kind of animal they have, they
   - ☐ a. laugh.
   - ☐ b. are angry.
   - ☐ c. are shocked.

7. How does the person who is telling the story seem to feel about the little animal?
   - ☐ a. He likes it.
   - ☐ b. He won't have anything to do with it.
   - ☐ c. He doesn't seem to care about it at all.

8. The fact that the storyteller considers the creature "almost one of the family" shows his
   - ☐ a. desire to have a little brother.
   - ☐ b. affection for the animal.
   - ☐ c. anger at the rest of his family.

The following passage, taken from the selection you have just read, has words omitted from it. Fill in each blank using a word from the set of five words in the column to the right of the passage. Check your answers using the Answer Key on page 205.

Dr. Ziemer arrived while we were still staring at the thing in the nest. He jumped out of his car and came running out to us in the backyard. He was wearing a red bathrobe over his _____ ,
and he looked pretty excited.

He ran up to the _____
and looked in. His eyes opened up wide and he knelt down on the ground and stared and stared and stared. After a long while he said softly, "That's it. By George, that's just what it is." Then he
_____ for another long
time and finally he shook his head and said, "It can't be true, but there it is."

He got up off his _____
and looked around at us. His eyes were just sparkling, he was so excited. He put his hand on my shoulder, and I could
_____ he was quiver-
ing. "An amazing thing's happened," he said, in a kind of _____ .
"I don't know how to account for it. It must be some sort of freak biological mixup that might happen once in a thousand years."

1. a. coat   b. clothes   c. underwear
    d. pajamas   e. suit

2. a. backyard   b. car   c. nest
    d. hole   e. house

3. a. looked   b. slept   c. stared
    d. thought   e. watched

4. a. car   b. ground   c. seat
    d. chair   e. knees

5. a. feel   b. sense   c. see
    d. watch   e. know

6. a. smile   b. yell   c. whisper
    d. excitement   e. way

"But what is it?" I asked.

Dr. Ziemer turned and pointed a trembling finger at the nest. "Believe it or not, you people have hatched out a

_____ ."
7

We just looked at him.

"Sound incredible, I know," he said, "and I can't explain it, but there it is. I've seen too many Triceratops skulls to be mistaken about this one."

"But—but how could it be a dinosaur?" Pop asked.

"Goodness gracious!" Mom spluttered. "And right here in our

_____ . It doesn't
8

seem hardly right. And on a Sunday, too."

7. a. dinosaur   b. Triceratops   c. thing
   d. egg   e. chicken

8. a. backyard   b. town   c. home
   d. community   e. nest

VOCABULARY

Look at the word in boldface in each exercise that follows and read carefully the sentence with it. Put an *x* in the box before the best meaning or synonym for the word as it is used in the sentence. Check your answers using the Answer Key on page 205.

1. His eyes were just **sparkling**, he was so excited.
   □ a. very cold
   □ b. very bright
   □ c. very sleepy

2. He put his hand on my shoulder, and I could feel he was **quivering**.
   □ a. thinking
   □ b. shaking
   □ c. ready to run

3. It must be some sort of freak **biological** mixup . . . you people have hatched out a dinosaur.
   - ☐ a. having to do with legal matters
   - ☐ b. having to do with family relationships
   - ☐ c. having to do with living things

4. Dr. Ziemer turned and pointed a **trembling** finger at the nest.
   - ☐ a. bleeding
   - ☐ b. shaking
   - ☐ c. unmoving

5. "Sounds **incredible**, I know," he said, "and I can't explain it."
   - ☐ a. common
   - ☐ b. reasonable
   - ☐ c. unbelievable

6. "I've seen too many Triceratops **skulls** to be mistaken about this one."
   - ☐ a. shells
   - ☐ b. feet
   - ☐ c. head bones

7. "Goodness gracious!" Mom **spluttered**.
   - ☐ a. spoke in a confused way
   - ☐ b. shouted loudly
   - ☐ c. whispered softly

8. She acted a little **dazed** at first, but pretty soon she followed the other hens. . . .
   - ☐ a. mixed up
   - ☐ b. unhappy
   - ☐ c. excited

A Good Friend Is...

Kathy Burch Johnson

Reading Time ☐ ☐ Maze

Comprehension ☐ ☐ Vocabulary

"A Good Friend Is . . ." by Kathy Burch
Johnson celebrates some of the characteristics
of a good friendship. After reading this article,
think about some of the important things
you share with your own good friends.

It seems like Julie and I have always known each other. I used to go over to her house before and after school because my mom worked.

We'd walk to school together. In the winter, we played mind games trying to convince ourselves that we weren't cold.

After school, we'd make a big batch of popcorn, watch television, or play house in her backyard. We sunbathed, walked to the store to buy ice cream, and talked and giggled for hours.

For one brief period we didn't see or write to each other much because we had both moved.

A few weeks before I was to leave for college, Julie called me. She told me that she had just been accepted to the same college I was going to. We were both so excited! We ended up in dorms near each other. We spent many hours of our freshman year talking, laughing, and catching up on each other's lives.

Now we see each other a couple of times a month. Although our lives are different, I still consider her one of my closest friends. We really value our friendship and we've *tried* to stay friends for so long. Ralph Waldo Emerson once said, "A friend may well be reckoned the masterpiece of nature." But being a good friend doesn't just happen. It takes some thought and work. Here are some characteristics of a good friend.

A good friend is supportive. This means through bad times and *good*. Supporting your friends also means accepting them for what and who they are. They don't have to feel exactly the same way you do about everything.

A good friend is loyal. Julie brings out the best in me. But she doesn't give up on me when I'm at my worst. She doesn't talk about my bad points with other people. Still, loyalty shouldn't blind you if your friend is doing something that will harm him or her. Loyalty means getting help for your friend.

A good friend knows how to share. Sharing means giving of yourself. And accepting what others share with you. Julie and I have shared our triumphs and tragedies for years. It is a joy to find someone who thinks like you do. To discover that, however, you must share your thoughts with another.

A good friend is trustworthy. The ability to keep confidences was the most important aspect of friendship in a survey I read. Trust also means that you know your friend wouldn't encourage you to do something wrong. He (or she) knows you won't lie to him or laugh at him.

Are you a good friend—a "masterpiece"?

Like most of us, you're probably only partly finished. And you see room for improvement. Think about the points that are important to you.

If you have good friends who have some or all of these traits, tell them how important their friendship is to you. You know, I think I just might go call Julie.

COMPREHENSION

Read the following questions and statements. For each one, put an *x* in the box before the option that contains the most complete or accurate answer. Check your answers using the Answer Key on page 205.

1. The girls went to Julie's house because
   - ☐ a. they walked to school together.
   - ☐ b. it was cold outside.
   - ☐ c. the author's mom worked.

2. For a short time they didn't see each other because
   - ☐ a. they were in different grades.
   - ☐ b. both girls moved away.
   - ☐ c. the girls had an argument.

3. Which phrase was *not* mentioned as a characteristic of a good friend?
   - ☐ a. sharing thoughts
   - ☐ b. gossiping about other friends
   - ☐ c. trusting each other

4. It is important to tell a friend
   - ☐ a. to transfer to your college.
   - ☐ b. how important the friendship is.
   - ☐ c. that you like someone else better.

5. The two girls are still friends because they
   - ☐ a. work at the same job.
   - ☐ b. work at keeping the friendship strong.
   - ☐ c. went to college together.

6. Another title for this article could be
   - ☐ a. A Celebration of Friendship.
   - ☐ b. After School Fun.
   - ☐ c. College Stories.

7. To be true friends, two people must
   - ☐ a. think alike.
   - ☐ b. enjoy going to parties.
   - ☐ c. share both good and bad times together.

8. The writer of this article is going to phone her friend because she
   - ☐ a. has realized again how valuable Julie is.
   - ☐ b. wants to talk about childhood memories.
   - ☐ c. needs Julie's advice about the article.

The following passage, taken from the selection you have just read, has words omitted from it. Fill in each blank using a word from the set of five words in the column to the right of the passage. Check your answers using the Answer Key on page 205.

Here are some characteristics of a good friend.

A good _____ is supportive. This means through bad times and *good*. _____ your friends also means accepting them for what and who they are. They don't have to feel exactly the same way you do about everything.

A good friend is _____. Julie brings out the best in me. But she doesn't give up on me when I'm at my worst. She doesn't talk about my bad points with other people. Still, loyalty shouldn't blind you if your friend is doing something that will _____ him or her. Loyalty means getting help for your friend.

A good friend knows how to share. _____ means giving of yourself. And accepting what others share with you. Julie and I have shared our triumphs and tragedies for years. It is a joy to find someone who thinks like you do. To discover that, however, you must share your _____ with another.

1. a. friendship   b. college   c. friend
    d. masterpiece   e. family

2. a. Being   b. Loving   c. Supporting
    d. Accepting   e. Knowing

3. a. loyal   b. lasting   c. important
    d. harmless   e. accepting

4. a. harm   b. hurt   c. anger
    d. forget   e. upset

5. a. Friendship   b. Affection   c. Caring
    d. Unselfishness   e. Sharing

6. a. things   b. thoughts   c. toys
    d. truths   e. ideas

A good friend is trustworthy. The ability to keep confidences was the most important aspect of _____ in a survey

₇

I read. Trust also means that you know your friend wouldn't encourage you to do something _____ .

₈

He (or she) knows you won't lie to him or laugh at him.

7. a. trust b. loyalty c. friendship
d. sharing   e. cooperation

8. a. silly b. embarrassing c. harmful
d. wrong e. dangerous

VOCABULARY

Look at the word in boldface in each exercise that follows and read carefully the sentence with it. Put an *x* in the box before the best meaning or synonym for the word as it is used in the sentence. Check your answers using the Answer Key on page 205.

1. In the winter, we played mind games trying to **convince** ourselves that we weren't cold.
   - ☐ a. point out differences
   - ☐ b. talk oneself into something
   - ☐ c. be in charge of

2. We really **value** our friendship and we've tried to stay friends for so long.
   - ☐ a. prize
   - ☐ b. ruin
   - ☐ c. accept

3. "A friend may well be reckoned the **masterpiece** of nature."
   - ☐ a. best work
   - ☐ b. first plan
   - ☐ c. special direction

4. **Supporting** your friends also means accepting them for what they are.
   - ☐ a. concentrating
   - ☐ b. expecting
   - ☐ c. helping

5. . . . **loyalty** shouldn't blind you if your friend is doing something that will harm him or her.
   - ☐ a. trust
   - ☐ b. affection
   - ☐ c. faithfulness

6. Julie and I have shared our **triumphs** and tragedies for years.
   - ☐ a. victories
   - ☐ b. sadnesses
   - ☐ c. angers

7. The ability to keep **confidences** was the most important aspect of friendship in a survey I read.
   - ☐ a. surprises
   - ☐ b. secrets
   - ☐ c. friends

8. If you have good friends who have some or all of these **traits**, tell them how important their friendship is to you.
   - ☐ a. characters
   - ☐ b. abilities
   - ☐ c. characteristics

The Cartoonist

Betsy Byars

Reading Time [ ]   [ ] Maze

Comprehension [ ]   [ ] Vocabulary

The Cartoonist by Betsy Byars tells the story
of several children who become involved in
a very special project. If you are interested
in reading more of this book, ask for it
at your school or public library.

Hey, Lizabeth!" Tree Parker yelled. "Take my picture. Take a picture of me and Alfie."

Alfie said, "Oh, come on, Tree, will you? I got to get home. I got to study." It was after school, and Alfie was eager to get to his drawing.

"Well, can't you wait just one minute? I want Lizabeth to take our picture. Oh, Liz-a-beth!"

Alfie and Tree were standing on the sidewalk in front of Elizabeth Elner's house. Elizabeth was posing her cat on the front steps. The cat had on a doll hat and sweater. Elizabeth was spending a lot of time getting the angle of the hat just right. She ignored Alfie and Tree.

"All right, Lizabeth, we're going to leave," Tree warned. "This is your last chance to take our pictures." Tree loved to have his picture taken. The people he envied most in the world were the people at football games who managed to jump in front of the TV camera and wave.

Elizabeth stepped back and took a long critical look at the cat. "Now, don't you move," she warned. She looked through the lens of the camera and got the cat in focus.

"Watch this," Tree whispered to Alfie. He began sneaking up the front walk.

Tree had gotten his nickname in second grade when he had taken the part of a weeping willow in an ecology play. Not until the class saw him standing there, wrapped in brown paper, artificial leaves in his hair, did they realize how much like a tree he was. Now no one—not even the teacher—called him anything else.

Slowly, his long arms and legs angling out, glancing back to see if Alfie was watching, Tree moved closer to Elizabeth and the cat.

Apparently unaware, Elizabeth said, "Because if this picture comes out, I'm going to enter it in the Purina cat contest."

Tree slipped closer to the steps. Just as Elizabeth was ready to snap the picture, he jumped forward, arms out, and said, "Scat!"

The startled cat jumped to the sidewalk and disappeared in the bushes.

Elizabeth spun around. Her face was red. "*Now* look what you've done, Tree. If that cat snags my sister's good doll sweater, you're going to get it."

"Oh, am I scared," Tree said. His limbs trembled.

"I mean it, Tree Parker."

"Come on, Tree," Alfie said. "I got to get home."

Elizabeth advanced. "If that cat comes back without his outfit—my sister only let me use it because I promised nothing would happen to it—and if he comes home without it, Tree . . ."

"What you going to do?"

"Let's *go*," Alfie said.

"Well, I want to find out what she's going to do. What you going to do, Lizabeth?"

"Just wait and see."

"Come *on*." Alfie grabbed Tree by the sleeve and pulled him away. Reluctantly Tree began to walk down the sidewalk.

"I wouldn't let her take my picture now if she got down on her knees and begged," he said.

COMPREHENSION

Read the following questions and statements. For each one, put an *x* in the box before the option that contains the most complete or accurate answer. Check your answers using the Answer Key on page 205.

1. Tree wanted Elizabeth to
   - ☐ a. take his picture.
   - ☐ b. study with him after school.
   - ☐ c. pose her cat differently.

2. Elizabeth was
   - ☐ a. playing with a doll.
   - ☐ b. standing in front of her house.
   - ☐ c. drawing pictures.

3. Alfie wanted to go home because he
   - ☐ a. did not feel well.
   - ☐ b. wanted to have his picture taken.
   - ☐ c. needed time to draw.

4. Tree had gotten his nickname because he
   - ☐ a. spent most of his time climbing trees.
   - ☐ b. knew a lot about trees.
   - ☐ c. once was a tree in a play.

5. Elizabeth is not interested in
   - ☐ a. Tree and Alfie.
   - ☐ b. her cat.
   - ☐ c. photography.

6. Tree envied people on television because he
   - ☐ a. wanted to be on camera.
   - ☐ b. enjoyed football games.
   - ☐ c. hoped to become a professional actor.

7. The cat's outfit
   - ☐ a. was old and shabby.
   - ☐ b. was Elizabeth's prize possession.
   - ☐ c. did not belong to Elizabeth.

8. Tree scared the cat in order to
   - ☐ a. impress Alfie.
   - ☐ b. annoy Elizabeth.
   - ☐ c. jump in front of the camera.

The following passage, taken from the selection you have just read, has words omitted from it. Fill in each blank using a word from the set of five words in the column to the right of the passage. Check your answers using the Answer Key on page 205.

"Watch this," Tree whispered to Alfie. He began sneaking up the front walk.

Tree had gotten his

_____ in second grade
1

when he had taken the part of a weeping willow in an ecology play. Not until the class saw him standing there, wrapped in brown paper, artificial leaves in his hair, did they _____ how
2

much like a tree he was. Now no one— not even the teacher—called him

anything _____ .
3

Slowly, his long arms and

_____ angling out,
4

glancing back to see if Alfie was watching, Tree moved closer to Elizabeth

and the _____ .
5

Apparently unaware, Elizabeth said, "Because if this picture comes out, I'm going to enter it in the Purina cat contest."

Tree slipped closer to the steps. Just as Elizabeth was ready to snap the

_____ , he jumped
6

forward, arms out, and said, "Scat!"

The startled cat jumped to the sidewalk

and _____ in the bushes.
7

1. a. camera   b. cat   c. dream
       d. nickname   e. ideas

2. a. see   b. look   c. realize
       d. find   e. say

3. a. else   b. but   c. funny
       d. serious   e. normal

4. a. legs   b. fingers   c. hair
       d. body   e. neck

5. a. house   b. steps   c. porch
       d. cat   e. camera

6. a. twig   b. branch   c. picture
       d. shutter   e. finger

7. a. disappeared   b. ran   c. fell
       d. hid   e. went

Elizabeth spun around. Her

_____ was red.
8

8. a. cat   b. face   c. camera

     d. hair   e. mood

VOCABULARY

**Look at the word in boldface in each exercise that
follows and read carefully the sentence with it. Put an
x in the box before the best meaning or synonym for
the word as it is used in the sentence. Check your
answers using the Answer Key on page 205.**

1. It was after school, and Alfie was
   eager to get to his drawing.
   □ a. ordered
   □ b. impatient
   □ c. slow

2. Elizabeth was **posing** her cat on the
   front step.
   □ a. chasing
   □ b. rescuing
   □ c. positioning

3. Elizabeth was spending a lot of time
   getting the **angle** of the hat just right.
   □ a. top
   □ b. tilt
   □ c. ribbon

4. The people he **envied** most in the
   world were the people at football
   games who managed to jump up in
   front of the TV camera and wave.
   □ a. slightly resembled
   □ b. disliked
   □ c. was jealous of

5. Elizabeth stepped back and took a
   long **critical** look at the cat.
   □ a. judging
   □ b. surprised
   □ c. angry

6. Not until the class saw him standing
   there, wrapped in brown paper,
   artificial leaves in his hair, did they
   realize how much like a tree he was.
   □ a. colored
   □ b. new
   □ c. fake

7. . . . **glancing** back to see if Alfie was
   watching, Tree moved closer to
   Elizabeth and the cat.
   □ a. shouting
   □ b. looking
   □ c. crawling

8. The **startled** cat jumped to the sidewalk and disappeared in the bushes.
   □ a. sleeping
   □ b. relaxed
   □ c. surprised

Set Your Sails for Fun!

Jennifer Albert

Reading Time			Maze
Comprehension			Vocabulary

This article gives you a look at a day of ocean sailing. If you are interested in more information about sailing, ask the librarian at your school or public library.

Imagine yourself gazing up at a clear blue sky, soaking up the rays, and being gently rocked back and forth. You inhale fresh, clean air. You hear only the pounding of the surf in the distance. And only the lapping waves against the hull. There is absolutely nothing for miles around you except aqua-blue water.

Sailing, when done properly, can be thrilling and exhilarating. Or it can be one of the most relaxing and soothing sports there is. Sailing is one of the oldest sports.

Sailboats are designed in many different styles for varying purposes. Some people want to race, and so need a sleeker design, while others may want to simply cruise along at a slow pace.

There is a whole language that goes along with sailing and a sailor must know it. For example, on a common sailboat called a *sloop*, there are at least three different "sheets" or lines used to control the sails. There is a name for every line. The sailor must know each one.

Let's run through a day of ocean sailing. Usually, the day begins early so you can have time to set up and get out on the water while it's still smooth.

Setting up requires teamwork. Sails must be brought out, battens (long, rulerlike sticks) are put into the sails for support, the jib (forward sail) is attached to the forestay and the mainsail is fed into a groove on the mast. Food, water, and other supplies are brought on board. Soon the boat is ready to sail!

Finally you cast off the dock lines, come aboard, and you're off! Careful maneuvering is necessary inside the breakwater where there are usually quite a few other boats. But after you're out on the ocean, you're free!

The jib is hoisted (raised) at about this time, or sometimes before leaving the dock, depending on the wind conditions. The captain pulls her into a nice "reach," with the sail at right angles to the wind. Then you can sit back, relax, and get some sun.

There are often several good hours of sailing around on the ocean. It all depends on the wind conditions. The wind determines where you go, how many times you need to change direction, and how long you can stay out. Because the wind is a variable, careful planning is needed to allow enough time to reach your destination before dark. It is best not to be out on the ocean fighting your way back at or after sunset.

Coming in an hour or so before dusk also gives you time to dock the boat, take down the sails, pack up everything, and leave the boat "shipshape" before heading home.

At the end of the day, you feel relaxed, warm from the sun, and sleepy. You'll look back on the day and you'll probably remember each picture printed in your mind. You'll remember the sun on the waves, the sea gulls, the blue sky, and the water all around.

Read the following questions and statements. For each one, put an *x* in the box before the option that contains the most complete or accurate answer. Check your answers using the Answer Key on page 205.

1. The author describes sailing as
   - ☐ a. running.
   - ☐ b. soothing.
   - ☐ c. terrifying.

2. A *sloop* is a
   - ☐ a. common type of sailboat.
   - ☐ b. sail used only for racing.
   - ☐ c. kind of sailboat that is no longer made.

3. The jib is raised when
   - ☐ a. you cast off dock lines.
   - ☐ b. the captain comes aboard.
   - ☐ c. the wind conditions are right.

4. Reaching your destination before dark always requires
   - ☐ a. hours of sailing.
   - ☐ b. changing directions.
   - ☐ c. careful planning.

5. In the article, the author does *not* mention
   - ☐ a. racing.
   - ☐ b. cruising.
   - ☐ c. fishing.

6. A sailor must know the language of sailing because he or she must
   - ☐ a. understand other sailors.
   - ☐ b. pass an examination.
   - ☐ c. teach the captain the language.

7. Inside the breakwater, careful maneuvering is needed because
   - ☐ a. the breakwater is very wide.
   - ☐ b. you might hit another boat.
   - ☐ c. the water is very rough.

8. Sailing on the ocean after dark
   - ☐ a. is recommended by the author.
   - ☐ b. can be dangerous.
   - ☐ c. requires the use of many sails.

The following passage, taken from the selection you have just read, has words omitted from it. Fill in each blank using a word from the set of five words in the column to the right of the passage. Check your answers using the Answer Key on page 205.

Finally you cast off the dock lines, come aboard, and you're off! Careful maneuvering is necessary inside the breakwater where there are usually quite a few other boats. But after you're out on the _____ , you're free!

1. a. dock   b. ocean   c. boat
   d. breakwater   e. wind

The jib is hoisted (raised) at about this time, or sometimes before leaving the dock, depending on the wind _____ . The captain pulls her into a nice "reach," with the sail at right angles to the wind. Then you can sit back, relax, and get some sun.

2. a. direction   b. conditions   c. speed
   d. velocity   e. power

3. a. ship's   b. wind   c. ocean
   d. weather   e. crew's

There are often several good hours of sailing around on the ocean. It all depends on the _____ conditions. The wind determines where you go, how many times you need to change direction, and how long you can stay out. Because the wind is a variable, careful _____ is needed to allow enough time to reach your destination before _____ . It is best not to be out on the ocean fighting your way back at or after sunset.

4. a. sailing   b. hoisting   c. planning
   d. timing   e. maneuvering

5. a. sunrise   b. dusk   c. dark
   d. daybreak   e. stopping

Coming in an hour or so before dusk also gives you time to dock the boat, take down the sails, pack up everything, and leave the _____

6

"shipshape" before heading home.

At the end of the day, you feel relaxed, warm from the _____ ,

7

and sleepy. You'll look back on the day and you'll probably remember each picture printed in your mind. You'll remember the sun on the waves, the sea gulls, the blue sky, and the _____ all around.

8

6.   a. boat   b. dock   c. lines
        d. sails   e. angles

7.   a. ride   b. ocean   c. sun
        d. weather   e. wind

8.   a. boats   b. friends   c. crew
        d. water   e. fun

VOCABULARY

Look at the word in boldface in each exercise that follows and read carefully the sentence with it. Put an *x* in the box before the best meaning or synonym for the word as it is used in the sentence. Check your answers using the Answer Key on page 205.

1. You **inhale** fresh, clean air.
   - ☐ a. choke
   - ☐ b. hold back
   - ☐ c. breathe in

2. Sailing, when done properly, can be thrilling and **exhilarating**.
   - ☐ a. tiring
   - ☐ b. exciting
   - ☐ c. defeating

3. Some people want to race, and so need a **sleeker** design. . . .
   - ☐ a. smoother
   - ☐ b. wider
   - ☐ c. basic

4. . . . there are at least three different "sheets" or lines used to **control** the sails.
   - ☐ a. manage
   - ☐ b. change
   - ☐ c. put together

5. Setting up **requires** teamwork.
   - ☐ a. makes
   - ☐ b. pushes
   - ☐ c. needs

6. Careful **maneuvering** is necessary inside the breakwater where there are usually quite a few other boats.
   - ☐ a. skillful moving
   - ☐ b. active racing
   - ☐ c. gentle swaying

7. Because the wind is a variable, careful planning is needed to allow enough time to reach your **destination** before dark.
   - ☐ a. person who owns the boat
   - ☐ b. top speed
   - ☐ c. place where you are going

8. Coming in an hour or so before **dusk** also gives you time to dock the boat. . . .
   - ☐ a. midnight
   - ☐ b. just before dark
   - ☐ c. sunrise

A Bear Called Paddington

Michael Bond

Reading Time ▢ ▢ Maze

Comprehension ▢ ▢ Vocabulary

Mr. and Mrs. Brown first met Paddington on a railway platform. In fact, that was how he came to have such an unusual name for a bear, for Paddington was the name of the station.

The Browns were there to meet their daughter Judy, who was coming home from school for the holidays. It was a warm summer day and the station was crowded with people on their way to the seaside. Trains were whistling, taxis hooting, porters rushing about shouting at one another, and altogether there was so much noise that Mr. Brown, who saw him first, had to tell his wife several times before she understood.

"A *bear*? On Paddington station?" Mrs. Brown looked at her husband in amazement. "Don't be silly, Henry. There can't be!"

Mr. Brown adjusted his glasses. "But there is," he insisted. "I distinctly saw it. Over there—behind those mailbags. It was wearing a funny kind of hat."

Without waiting for a reply he caught hold of his wife's arm and pushed her through the crowd, round a trolley laden with chocolate and cups of tea, past a bookstall, and through a gap in a pile of suitcases towards the Lost Property Office.

"There you are," he announced, triumphantly, pointing towards a dark corner. "I told you so!"

Mrs. Brown followed the direction of his arm and dimly made out a small, furry object in the shadows. It seemed to be sitting on some kind of suitcase and around its neck there was a label with some writing on it. The suitcase was old and battered and on the side, in large letters, were the words WANTED ON VOYAGE.

Mrs. Brown clutched at her husband. "Why, Henry," she exclaimed. "I believe you were right after all. It *is* a bear!"

She peered at it more closely. It seemed a very unusual kind of bear. It was brown in color, a rather dirty brown, and it was wearing a most odd-looking hat, with a wide brim, just as Mr. Brown had said. From beneath the brim two large, round eyes stared back at her.

Seeing that something was expected of it the bear stood up and politely raised its hat, revealing two black ears. "Good afternoon," it said, in a small, clear voice.

"Er . . . good afternoon," replied Mr. Brown, doubtfully. There was a moment of silence.

The bear looked at them inquiringly. "Can I help you?"

Mr. Brown looked rather embarrassed. "Well . . . no. Er . . . as a matter of fact, we were wondering if we could help you."

Mrs. Brown bent down. "You're a very small bear," she said.

The bear puffed out its chest. "I'm a very rare sort of bear," he replied, importantly. "There aren't many of us left where I come from."

"And where is that?" asked Mrs. Brown.

The bear looked round carefully before replying. "Darkest Peru. I'm not really supposed to be here at all. I'm a stowaway!"

"A stowaway?" Mr. Brown lowered his voice and looked around anxiously.

COMPREHENSION

Read the following questions and statements. For each one, put an *x* in the box before the option that contains the most complete or accurate answer. Check your answers using the Answer Key on page 205.

1. Paddington was named after
   □ a. a ship.
   □ b. a train station.
   □ c. his father.

2. Paddington was wearing an odd-looking
   □ a. bow tie.
   □ b. hat.
   □ c. pair of glasses.

3. Paddington came from
   □ a. Peru.
   □ b. Africa.
   □ c. China.

4. The bear told the Browns that he was a
   □ a. first-class passenger.
   □ b. tourist.
   □ c. stowaway.

5. When Mrs. Brown first heard her husband talk about the bear she
   □ a. was uninterested.
   □ b. was frightened.
   □ c. did not believe him.

6. How did the Browns react when they met Paddington?
   □ a. They were surprised.
   □ b. They mistook him for their daughter.
   □ c. They hardly noticed him.

7. Paddington treated the Browns
   □ a. politely.
   □ b. rudely.
   □ c. unkindly.

8. The bear seemed to be
   □ a. unhappy with himself.
   □ b. disappointed with himself.
   □ c. proud of himself.

MAZE

The following passage, taken from the selection you have just read, has words omitted from it. Fill in each blank using a word from the set of five words in the column to the right of the passage. Check your answers using the Answer Key on page 205.

Mr. and Mrs. Brown first met Paddington on a railway platform. In fact, that was how he came to have such an unusual name for a

_____ , for Paddington was
₁

the name of the _____ .
₂

The Browns were there to meet their daughter Judy, who was coming home from school for the holidays. It was a warm summer day and the station was crowded with people on their way to the seaside. Trains were whistling, taxis hooting, porters rushing about shouting at one another, and altogether there was so

much _____ that Mr.
₃

Brown, who saw him first, had to tell his wife several times before she understood.

"A *bear*? On Paddington station?" Mrs. Brown looked at her

_____ in amazement.
₄

"Don't be silly, _____ .
₅

There can't be!"

Mr. Brown adjusted his glasses. "But there is," he insisted. "I distinctly saw it. Over there—behind those mailbags. It was wearing a funny kind of

_____ ."
₆

Without waiting for a reply he caught

1. a. platform   b. performer   c. school
   d. bear   e. holiday

2. a. train   b. station   c. area
   d. railway   e. daughter

3. a. trouble   b. sound   c. shouting
   d. noise   e. warmth

4. a. watch   b. ticket   c. husband
   d. daughter   e. suitcase

5. a. Mr. Brown   b. Judy   c. Peru
   d. Henry   e. Paddington

6. a. jacket   b. sign   c. hat
   d. vest   e. brim

hold of his wife's arm and pushed her through the crowd, round a trolley laden with chocolate and cups of tea, past a bookstall, and through a gap in a pile of suitcases towards the Lost Property Office.

"There you are," he announced, triumphantly, pointing towards a dark corner. "I told you so!"

Mrs. Brown followed the direction of his arm and dimly made out a small, furry object in the shadows. It seemed to be sitting on some kind of _____ and around its
₇
neck there was a label with some writing on it. The suitcase was old and battered and on the side, in large _____ , were the
₈
words WANTED ON VOYAGE.

7. a. suitcase   b. couch   c. rug
    d. mailbag   e. platform

8. a. crayon b. letters c. scribbles
    d. print e. size

VOCABULARY

Look at the word in boldface in each exercise that follows and read carefully the sentence with it. Put an *x* in the box before the best meaning or synonym for the word as it is used in the sentence. Check your answers using the Answer Key on page 205.

1. Mrs. Brown looked at her husband in **amazement**. "Don't be silly, Henry. There can't be!"
   ☐ a. anger
   ☐ b. fear
   ☐ c. surprise

2. "But there is," he insisted. "I **distinctly** saw it. Over there—behind those mailbags."
   ☐ a. very clearly
   ☐ b. doubtfully
   ☐ c. with difficulty

3. "There you are," he announced **triumphantly**, pointing towards a dark corner. "I told you so."
   - ☐ a. with a look of shame
   - ☐ b. with a tone of sadness
   - ☐ c. with a sense of victory

4. The suitcase was old and **battered**. . . .
   - ☐ a. heavy
   - ☐ b. well-worn
   - ☐ c. brand new

5. "Why, Henry," she **exclaimed**. "I believe you were right after all. It *is* a bear."
   - ☐ a. spoke excitedly
   - ☐ b. began to cry
   - ☐ c. whispered

6. She **peered** at it more closely. It was a very unusual kind of bear.
   - ☐ a. laughed
   - ☐ b. looked
   - ☐ c. studied

7. The bear looked at them **inquiringly**, "Can I help you?"
   - ☐ a. in a questioning way
   - ☐ b. with little interest
   - ☐ c. in a rude way

8. The bear puffed out its chest, "I'm a very rare sort of bear," he replied **importantly**."
   - ☐ a. with shyness
   - ☐ b. with pride
   - ☐ c. with embarrassment

Set 6

To See Half the World

Edward Fry

Reading Time [ ]   [ ] Maze

Comprehension [ ]   [ ] Vocabulary

This article shows you the exciting world that can open up to you when you learn to snorkel. If you are interested in more information about snorkeling, ask the librarian at your school or public library.

Most people who go to Florida or California see only half the world. They see the half above the water. To see the other half, you must learn to "snorkel."

First you have to learn to swim. It also helps to know how to float so you can rest. If you learn to float in a lake or in a swimming pool, you will easily float in the ocean because salt water holds you up better.

To snorkel, the only things you must have are a face mask and a snorkel tube. A snorkel tube is a short curved piece of plastic or rubber tubing that you put in your mouth so you can breathe while floating on your stomach. A face mask covers your eyes and nose. You can't see well under water unless your eyes are protected.

Now, to see the half of the world under water, all you have to do is float face down with your face mask on. To breathe, just put your snorkel in your mouth with the other end up in the air behind your head. For some reason or another this is scary for a lot of people. So in the beginning, just do it in shallow water where you can stand up if you get nervous. After a little while you will get used to breathing through your mouth while floating.

If a small wave should wash over the top of your snorkel tube, a little water can come down. Just stop breathing for a moment and give a good hard blow through the tube. The water and air will come flying out and you will look like a whale.

While you are floating with your face mask on you will notice that you can see the bottom and the things floating in the water. If you lose any money or your watch in the water a face mask will help you find it. And if there are any fish or interesting shells you will see them too.

Pretty soon you will get tired of floating in one spot and will want to see more. You can swim without even raising your head. The breaststroke works just fine while floating with your snorkel and face mask on. Or you can just kick your legs and you will move. If you really want to get somewhere put some swim fins on your feet and you will really travel.

After a little while you will get tired of just looking at a sandy bottom. Then you will want to see some fish and more interesting things. To see them, you need to be near rocks or seaweed. Single fish or schools of fish do show up almost anywhere in the ocean, but your chances of seeing them are low. However, in warmer water like Florida, California, or Mexico there are almost always some fish near rocks, seaweed, or sunken boats. And just looking at the rocks and seaweed under water can be a whole new seeing experience. Now you are seeing the half of the world that most people never see.

COMPREHENSION

Read the following questions and statements. For each one, put an x in the box before the option that contains the most complete or accurate answer. Check your answers using the Answer Key on page 206.

1. Most people are not familiar with
   - ☐ a. the world below the water.
   - ☐ b. the world above the water.
   - ☐ c. California or Florida.

2. A snorkel tube is used for
   - ☐ a. breathing air.
   - ☐ b. protecting your eyes.
   - ☐ c. floating on your stomach.

3. You will travel faster through the water if you wear
   - ☐ a. a face mask.
   - ☐ b. fins.
   - ☐ c. a snorkel.

4. You are more likely to see fish near
   - ☐ a. seaweed.
   - ☐ b. beaches.
   - ☐ c. sailboats.

5. Most people only see half the world because they
   - ☐ a. have not traveled to warmer climates.
   - ☐ b. stay out of the sun.
   - ☐ c. have not seen below the surface of the water.

6. This article tells you that snorkeling
   - ☐ a. is frightening and dangerous.
   - ☐ b. can only be done in shallow water.
   - ☐ c. will show you many interesting things.

7. The author probably
   - ☐ a. has never snorkeled.
   - ☐ b. enjoys snorkeling.
   - ☐ c. hates snorkeling.

8. Choose the best word to describe this article.
   - ☐ a. informative
   - ☐ b. humorous
   - ☐ c. mysterious

The following passage, taken from the selection you have just read, has words omitted from it. Fill in each blank using a word from the set of five words in the column to the right of the passage. Check your answers using the Answer Key on page 206.

Most people who go to Florida or California see only half the world. They see the half above the water. To see the other _____ 1 , you must learn to "snorkel."

First you have to learn to swim. It also helps to know how to float so you can rest. If you learn to float in a lake or in a swimming _____ 2 , you will easily float in the ocean because salt water holds you up better.

To snorkel, the only things you must have are a _____ 3 mask and a snorkel tube. A snorkel tube is a short curved piece of plastic or _____ 4 tubing that you put in your mouth so you can breathe while floating on your stomach. A face mask covers your eyes and nose. You can't see well under _____ 5 unless your eyes are protected.

Now, to see the half of the world under water, all you have to do is _____ 6 face down with your face mask on. To breathe, just put your snorkel in your

1. a. section   b. piece   c. land
      d. half   e. water

2. a. team   b. pool   c. club
      d. hole   e. pond

3. a. face   b. head   c. body
      d. eye   e. snorkel

4. a. glass   b. rubber   c. threaded
      d. bicycle   e. twisted

5. a. water   b. pressure   c. land
      d. sea   e. bottom

6. a. swim   b. float   c. walk
      d. surf   e. stand

mouth with the other end up in the

_____ behind your
        7

head. For some reason or another this is

scary for a lot of people. So in the

beginning, just do it in shallow water

where you can stand up if you get

nervous. After a little while you will get

used to breathing through your

_____ while
        8

floating.

7. a. space   b. water   c. hair
          d. area   e. air

8. a. mouth   b. nose   c. tube
          d. snorkel   e. mask

VOCABULARY

**Look at the word in boldface in each exercise that
follows and read carefully the sentence with it. Put an
x in the box before the best meaning or synonym for
the word as it is used in the sentence. Check your
answers using the Answer Key on page 206.**

1. You can't see well under water unless
   your eyes are **protected**.
   ☐ a. guarded
   ☐ b. attacked
   ☐ c. blurred

2. So in the beginning, just do it in very
   shallow water where you can stand up
   if you get nervous.
   ☐ a. very deep
   ☐ b. cool and clear
   ☐ c. not deep

3. If a small wave should **wash** over the
   top of your snorkel tube, a little water
   can come down.
   ☐ a. drown
   ☐ b. flow
   ☐ c. whisper

4. . . . floating with your face mask on you
   will **notice** that you can see the bottom
   and the things floating in the water.
   ☐ a. discover
   ☐ b. forget
   ☐ c. announce

5. The **breaststroke** works just fine while
   floating with your snorkel and face
   mask on.
   ☐ a. illness
   ☐ b. swimming move
   ☐ c. shout

6. Single fish or **schools** of fish do show
   up almost anywhere in the ocean.
   ☐ a. remains
   ☐ b. groups
   ☐ c. buildings

7. . . . there are almost always some fish near rocks, seaweed, or **sunken** boats.
   - ☐ a. fishing
   - ☐ b. lying on the bottom
   - ☐ c. floating on the top

8. And just looking at the rocks and seaweed under water can be a whole new kind of seeing **experience**.
   - ☐ a. boat
   - ☐ b. expert
   - ☐ c. event

Charlie and the Chocolate Factory

Roald Dahl

| Reading Time | | | Maze |
| Comprehension | | | Vocabulary |

The following passage was taken from *Charlie and the Chocolate Factory* by Roald Dahl. It is a story about five lucky children who get to see the inside of a chocolate factory. If you would like to read more, ask for this book at either your school or public library.

An important room, this!" cried Mr. Wonka, taking a bunch of keys from his pocket and slipping one into the keyhole of the door. "*This* is the nerve center of the whole factory, the heart of the whole business! And so *beautiful!*" I *insist* upon my rooms being beautiful! I can't *abide* ugliness in factories! *In* we go, then! But *do* be careful, my dear children! Don't lose your heads! Don't get overexcited! Keep very calm!"

Mr. Wonka opened the door. Five children and nine grownups pushed their ways in—and *oh,* what an amazing sight it was that now met their eyes!

They were looking down upon a lovely valley. There were green meadows on either side of the valley, and along the bottom of it there flowed a great brown river.

What is more, there was a tremendous waterfall halfway along the river—a steep cliff over which the water curled and rolled in a solid sheet, and then went crashing down into a boiling, churning whirlpool of froth and spray.

Below the waterfall (and this was the most astonishing sight of all), a whole mass of enormous glass pipes were dangling down into the river from somewhere high up in the ceiling! They really were *enormous,* those pipes. There

must have been a dozen of them at least, and they were sucking up the brownish muddy water from the river and carrying it away to goodness knows where. And because they were made of glass, you could see the liquid flowing and bubbling along inside them, and above the noise of the waterfall, you could hear the never-ending suck-suck-sucking sound of the pipes as they did their homework.

Graceful trees and bushes were growing along the riverbanks—weeping willows and alders and tall clumps of rhododendrons with their pink and red and mauve blossoms. In the meadows there were thousands of buttercups.

"*There!*" cried Mr. Wonka, dancing up and down and pointing his gold-topped cane at the great brown river. "It's *all* chocolate!" Every drop of that river is hot melted chocolate of the finest quality. The *very* finest quality. There's enough chocolate in there to fill *every* bathtub in the *entire* country! *And* all the swimming pools as well! Isn't it *terrific?* And just look at my pipes! They suck up the chocolate and carry it away to all the other rooms in the factory where it is needed! Thousands of gallons an hour, my dear children! Thousands and thousands of gallons!"

The children and their parents were too

flabbergasted to speak. They were staggered. They were dumbfounded. They were bewildered and dazzled. They were completely bowled over by the hugeness of the whole thing. They simply stood and stared.

"The waterfall is *most* important!" Mr. Wonka went on. "It mixes the chocolate! It churns it up! It pounds it and beats it! It makes it light and frothy! No other factory in the world mixes its chocolate by waterfall!"

COMPREHENSION

Read the following questions and statements. For each one, put an *x* in the box before the option that contains the most complete or accurate answer. Check your answers using the Answer Key on page 206.

1. The most important room in Mr. Wonka's factory is the
   - ☐ a. visitors' room.
   - ☐ b. chocolate room.
   - ☐ c. office.

2. How many children go with Mr. Wonka into the room?
   - ☐ a. two
   - ☐ b. three
   - ☐ c. five

3. The river contains
   - ☐ a. melted chocolate.
   - ☐ b. salt water.
   - ☐ c. fresh milk.

4. The pipes in the room
   - ☐ a. make a sucking sound.
   - ☐ b. carry the chocolate to other parts of the factory.
   - ☐ c. both a and b

5. Mr. Wonka seems to be
   - ☐ a. bored with the children.
   - ☐ b. sad about the weather.
   - ☐ c. excited about the chocolate room.

6. When Mr. Wonka talks about his factory he acts very
   - ☐ a. ashamed.
   - ☐ b. proud.
   - ☐ c. secretive.

7. The factory is
   - ☐ a. an ugly place to be in.
   - ☐ b. beautifully decorated.
   - ☐ c. closed for vacation.

8. The visitors probably
   - ☐ a. have never seen a factory like this one.
   - ☐ b. often visit chocolate factories.
   - ☐ c. don't like the factory at all.

The following passage, taken from the selection you have just read, has words omitted from it. Fill in each blank using a word from the set of five words in the column to the right of the passage. Check your answers using the Answer Key on page 206.

"An important room, this!" cried Mr. Wonka, taking a bunch of _____ from his pocket and slipping one into the keyhole of the door. "This is the nerve center of the whole factory, the heart of the whole business! And so _____!" I insist upon my rooms being beautiful! I can't abide ugliness in factories! In we go, then! But do be careful, my dear children! Don't lose your heads! Don't get overexcited! Keep very calm!"

Mr. Wonka opened the _____. Five children and nine grownups pushed their ways in— and oh, what an amazing sight it was that now met their eyes!

They were looking down upon a lovely _____. There were green meadows on either side of the valley, and along the bottom of it there flowed a great brown _____.

What is more, there was a tremendous waterfall halfway along the river—a steep cliff over which the water curled and rolled in a solid sheet, and then went crashing

1. a. candy   b. change   c. sweets
        d. coins   e. keys

2. a. ugly   b. busy   c. beautiful
        d. lovely   e. exciting

3. a. factory   b. door   c. business
        d. gate   e. keyhole

4.   a. sight   b. river   c. cliff
        d. meadow   e. valley

5.   a. river   b. road   c. liquid
        d. waterway   e. lake

down into a boiling, churning whirlpool of froth and spray.

Below the _____
6
(and this was the most astonishing sight of all), a whole mass of enormous _____ pipes were
7
dangling down into the river from somewhere high up in the ceiling! They really were enormous, those _____ . There must
8
have been a dozen of them at least, and they were sucking up the brownish muddy water from the river and carrying it away to goodness knows where. And because they were made of glass, you could see the liquid flowing and bubbling along inside them.

6. a. cliff   b. whirlpool   c. waterfall
   d. ceiling   e. river

7. a. chocolate   b. glass   c. mud
   d. liquid   e. froth

8. a. bubbles   b. masses   c. pipes
   d. ceilings   e. waterfalls

VOCABULARY

Look at the word in boldface in each exercise that follows and read carefully the sentence with it. Put an *x* in the box before the best meaning or synonym for the word as it is used in the sentence. Check your answers using the Answer Key on page 206.

1. "I insist upon my rooms being beautiful! I can't **abide** ugliness in factories!"
   ☐ a. put up with
   ☐ b. think about
   ☐ c. demand

2. What is more, there was a **tremendous** waterfall halfway along the river. . . .
   ☐ a. huge
   ☐ b. low
   ☐ c. shallow

3. . . . and then went crashing down into a boiling, **churning** whirlpool of froth and spray.
   ☐ a. very calm and smooth
   ☐ b. turning over lightly
   ☐ c. moving as if shaken

4. . . . weeping willows and alders and tall clumps of **rhododendrons** with their pink and red and mauve blossoms.
   ☐ a. a kind of grass
   ☐ b. small vegetable plants
   ☐ c. flowering bushes

5. "Every drop of that river is hot melted chocolate of the finest **quality**."
   ☐ a. fame
   ☐ b. kind
   ☐ c. number

6. "There's enough chocolate in there to fill every bathtub in the **entire** country!"
   ☐ a. all and more
   ☐ b. whole
   ☐ c. section

7. The children and their parents were too **flabbergasted** to speak.
   ☐ a. happy
   ☐ b. hungry
   ☐ c. surprised

8. "It pounds and beats it! It makes it light and **frothy**!"
   ☐ a. foamy
   ☐ b. boiling
   ☐ c. solid

They Study the Ocean

Melvin Berger

Reading Time ☐   ☐ Maze

Comprehension ☐   ☐ Vocabulary

This article is from a book called *Jobs That Save Our Environment* by Melvin Berger. The book describes some of the important jobs that help to preserve our natural world. If you are interested in reading more of this book, ask for it at your school or public library.

Holger Jannasch could not believe his eyes. A baloney sandwich that had been soaking in a lunch box at the bottom of the sea for nearly a year looked almost as good as when it was fresh. The sandwich had not spoiled or become rotten. The germs, or bacteria, in the sea had not broken down the food as he had expected.

Jannasch is a *marine biologist*. He studies living things in the seas. He wondered why the bacteria in the water had not spoiled the sandwich.

He set up an experiment in which he grew bacteria in two groups of bottles. He put one group of bacteria-filled bottles into the sea. The other group he kept in the laboratory.

The results showed that bacteria decompose waste materials faster on land than they do in seawater. That explained why the food had not spoiled in seawater.

Marine biologists are not only concerned with bacteria. They are also interested in every form of life found in the sea. Sometimes they work out at sea, on a research ship or submarine. Or sometimes they work on shore in laboratories.

Elizabeth Bunce is a *marine geophysicist*. She studies the structure and shape of the ocean floor, the rocks and mud that are found there. And she studies the deeper structure beneath the sea floor.

Elizabeth Bunce wants to know more about the shape of the ocean bottom. She wants to learn about the mountains, valleys, and ridges that crisscross the bottom of the sea. When she is on a research ship, she uses a machine that produces loud sounds under the water. By seeing how long it takes for the echo of the sound to bounce off the bottom, she can tell the depth of the water. Then maps and charts can be drawn of the sea bottom.

Marine chemists do research on the chemicals in seawater. Sometimes they work at sea, collecting and testing samples of water. Other times, they do research in a shore laboratory.

Physical oceanographers study ocean currents, waves, and tides. Each year they drop thousands of drift bottles into the water from research ships. They want to see where the bottles are carried by the ocean currents. Using drift bottles and other tools, they have been able to trace most of the currents in the oceans of the world.

There are about six thousand *oceanographers* in the United States. About three hundred are women. They are all college graduates. Most hold advanced degrees in science. The largest number work at university or government laboratories. A few work for private industries. They design new tools for marine science and do research.

People who work in oceanography like the adventure and challenge of the sea. Always changing and always moving, the sea does not give up its secrets easily. The sea batters their ships. It sometimes destroys their tools. It often makes them seasick. But for the person who loves the sea and is interested in science, oceanography is a most rewarding and satisfying career.

COMPREHENSION

Read the following questions and statements. For each one, put an *x* in the box before the option that contains the most complete or accurate answer. Check your answers using the Answer Key on page 206.

1. The baloney sandwich
   - ☐ a. was rotten.
   - ☐ b. looked nearly fresh.
   - ☐ c. did not surprise Holger Jannasch.

2. A marine geophysicist studies
   - ☐ a. marine bacteria.
   - ☐ b. chemicals in seawater.
   - ☐ c. the ocean floor.

3. Drift bottles are used to
   - ☐ a. measure bacteria.
   - ☐ b. follow ocean currents.
   - ☐ c. fight seasickness.

4. Oceanographers
   - ☐ a. design new tools for marine science.
   - ☐ b. never work in laboratories.
   - ☐ c. bounce echoes off the ocean bottom.

5. A marine biologist
   - ☐ a. does not need a college degree.
   - ☐ b. is interested in living things.
   - ☐ c. drops thousands of drift bottles.

6. The article points out that
   - ☐ a. oceanography is a dangerous career.
   - ☐ b. few scholarships are available on the university level.
   - ☐ c. more men than women become oceanographers.

7. Marine scientists work
   - ☐ a. on land and on the ocean.
   - ☐ b. only on the ocean.
   - ☐ c. only on land.

8. When the author says that "the sea does not give up its secrets easily," he means that
   - ☐ a. studying the sea requires hard work.
   - ☐ b. new research tools must be designed.
   - ☐ c. we have nothing more to learn from the sea.

The following passage, taken from the selection you have just read, has words omitted from it. Fill in each blank using a word from the set of five words in the column to the right of the passage. Check your answers using the Answer Key on page 206.

Holger Jannasch could not believe his eyes. A baloney sandwich that had been soaking in a lunch box at the bottom of the sea for nearly a year looked almost as good as when it was fresh. The sandwich had not _____ or become rotten. The germs, or bacteria, in the sea had not broken down the food as he had expected.

1. a. spoiled   b. melted   c. decayed
   d. imploded   e. rotted

Jannasch is a *marine biologist*. He studies living things in the _____ . He wondered why the bacteria in the water had not spoiled the _____ .

2. a. marina   b. sandwiches   c. seas
   d. bacteria   e. laboratory

3. a. food   b. baloney   c. sandwich
   d. lunch box   e. meal

He set up an experiment in which he grew _____ in two groups of bottles. He put one group of bacteria-filled bottles into the sea. The other group he kept in the laboratory.

4. a. seaweed   b. plants   c. food
   d. bacteria   e. germs

The results showed that bacteria decompose waste materials faster on land than they do in _____ . That explained why the food had not spoiled in seawater.

5. a. food   b. laboratories   c. air
   d. sandwiches   e. seawater

Marine biologists are not only concerned with bacteria. They are also interested in every form of life found in the sea. Sometimes they work out at sea, on a research ship or submarine. Or sometimes they work on shore in laboratories.

Elizabeth Bunce is a *marine geophysicist*. She studies the structure and shape of the ocean floor, the rocks and mud that are found there. And she studies the deeper structure beneath the sea

_____ .
6

Elizabeth Bunce wants to know

_____ about the shape
7

of the _____ bottom.
8

6. a. floor   b. level   c. rocks

d. structure   e. life

7. a. less   b. that   c. nothing

d. more   e. how

8. a. ocean   b. laboratory   c. mountain

d. university   e. chemical

VOCABULARY

Look at the word in boldface in each exercise that follows and read carefully the sentence with it. Put an *x* in the box before the best meaning or synonym for the word as it is used in the sentence. Check your answers using the Answer Key on page 206.

1. He set up an **experiment** in which he grew bacteria in two groups of bottles.
   - ☐ a. idea
   - ☐ b. test
   - ☐ c. puzzle

2. The results showed that bacteria **decompose** waste materials faster on land than they do in seawater.
   - ☐ a. swallow
   - ☐ b. find
   - ☐ c. rot

3. That explained why the food was not **spoiled** in seawater.
   - ☐ a. improved
   - ☐ b. ruined
   - ☐ c. diseased

4. Sometimes they work out at sea on a **research** ship or submarine.
   - ☐ a. military
   - ☐ b. study
   - ☐ c. pleasure

5. She studies the **structure** and shape of the ocean floor, the rocks and mud that are found there.
   - ☐ a. way something is built
   - ☐ b. type of marine rock
   - ☐ c. laboratory

6. Sometimes they work at sea, collecting and testing **samples** of water.
   - ☐ a. large quantities
   - ☐ b. small amounts
   - ☐ c. without chemicals

7. Using drift bottles and other tools, they have been able to **trace** most of the currents in the oceans of the world.
   - ☐ a. build
   - ☐ b. design
   - ☐ c. track

8. But for the person that loves the sea and is interested in science, oceanography is a most rewarding and **satisfying** career.
   - ☐ a. enjoyable
   - ☐ b. dull
   - ☐ c. difficult

Hotel for Dogs

Lois Duncan

Reading Time ▢ ▢ Maze

Comprehension ▢ ▢ Vocabulary

Hotel for Dogs by Lois Duncan tells about
the problems a girl faces when she decides to fix
up a vacant house for a family of stray dogs. If
you are interested in reading more of this book,
ask for it at your school or public library.

Thank goodness, it's Friday," Liz said. "This way I can spend all tomorrow over here getting them settled. Oh, Bruce, this is the most wonderful idea! Sadie and her puppies will think they're staying in a hotel!"

"Well, they had better not get too used to it," Bruce said. "As soon as the pups are old enough, we're going to find homes for every one of them and for Sadie too."

He spoke decisively to cover the fact that he was beginning to feel a little nervous. The idea had seemed so reasonable when it had first occurred to him: a vacant house with no one to tend it, four little dogs that needed a place to stay, so why not put them together for a few weeks?

The thing that was not reasonable was the way Liz was acting. In the day she had spent at home having her stomachache, she had formed a deep attachment for the group in the sewing closet. She had given them all names—Sadie for the mother and Tom, Dick, and Harry for the puppies—and she was acting as though she expected to be their mistress for the rest of her life.

"This is just an emergency thing, Liz," Bruce kept saying, as he followed her about. "This is somebody's else's property, even if they're not living here.

We really shouldn't be using it at all."

"I know, I know." Liz's eyes were shining with excitement. "I think Sadie would like the pink bedroom at the front of the hotel, don't you? We can fix her a bed in the corner, and when the puppies start walking they can go exploring down the hall to the living room."

"By the time they can do that, they'll be ready to leave," Bruce said. "We should start right now trying to line up homes for them. Does your school have a bulletin board? You could pin up a sort of announcement—"

But Liz was gone again, hurrying through to the kitchen to see if the faucets were working.

Liz was up at dawn the next morning and out of the house before anyone else was awake. Mrs. Walker discovered her room empty when she went to call her to breakfast.

"I can't understand it," she said in bewilderment, as she joined the rest of the family in the dining room. "Liz never gets up early if she can help it. Where in the world could she have disappeared to?"

"Perhaps she's gone to someone's house," Mr. Walker suggested. "She talks as though she has plenty of school friends she likes to play with."

"This early?" Mrs. Walker shook her

head. "Nobody goes visiting before breakfast." She turned to Bruce. "Did your sister say anything to you about having plans for this morning?"

"I—I don't think so. I mean, I don't exactly remember." Bruce felt his face growing hot. He had never been able to tell a lie successfully, even a little one.

COMPREHENSION

Read the following questions and statements. For each one, put an *x* in the box before the option that contains the most complete or accurate answer. Check your answers using the Answer Key on page 206.

1. After learning about Liz's plan, Bruce felt
   □ a. excited.
   □ b. nervous.
   □ c. sick.

2. Liz wanted Sadie's room to be
   □ a. near the hall.
   □ b. in the living room.
   □ c. at the front of the hotel.

3. Liz disappeared
   □ a. after dinner.
   □ b. during lunch.
   □ c. before breakfast.

4. Bruce found it difficult to
   □ a. find the hotel.
   □ b. tell a lie.
   □ c. talk to Liz.

5. Liz chose the hotel because
   □ a. the rent was affordable.
   □ b. it was nearby.
   □ c. no one lived there.

6. Liz showed her attachment to the dogs by
   □ a. keeping them in the sewing closet.
   □ b. giving them names.
   □ c. posting an announcement about them.

7. Bruce feared that Liz would
   □ a. harm the dogs.
   □ b. ask him to paint the hotel.
   □ c. not be able to give the dogs away.

8. Mrs. Walker was beginning to get
   □ a. suspicious.
   □ b. dizzy.
   □ c. angry.

The following passage, taken from the selection you have just read, has words omitted from it. Fill in each blank using a word from the set of five words in the column to the right of the passage. Check your answers using the Answer Key on page 206.

"This is just an emergency thing, Liz," Bruce kept saying, as he followed her about. "This is somebody's else's property, even if they're not _____ here. We really shouldn't be using it at all."

"I know, I _____ ." Liz's eyes were shining with excitement. "I think Sadie would like the pink bedroom at the front of the hotel, don't you? We can fix her a _____ in the corner, and when the puppies start walking they can go exploring down the hall to the living room."

"By the time they can do that, they'll be ready to leave," Bruce said. "We should start right now trying to line up _____ for them. Does your school have a _____ board? You could pin up a sort of announcement—"

But Liz was gone again, hurrying through to the _____ to see if the faucets were working.

Liz was up at dawn the next _____ and out of the house before anyone else was _____ .

1. a. renting b. staying c. living
    d. happy e. watching

2. a. understood b. know c. see
    d. can e. think

3. a. meal b. snack c. place
    d. room e. bed

4. a. bottles b. homes c. kids
    d. rooms e. places

5. a. chalk b. flashing c. score
    d. bulletin e. school

6. a. kitchen b. sink c. tub
    d. washer e. hose

7. a. night b. afternoon c. morning
    d. breakfast e. week

8. a. aware b. around c. alone
    d. alert e. awake

**Look at the word in boldface in each exercise that
follows and read carefully the sentence with it. Put an
x in the box before the best meaning or synonym for
the word as it is used in the sentence. Check your
answers using the Answer Key on page 206.**

1. He spoke **decisively** to cover the
   fact that he was beginning to
   get a little nervous.
   - □ a. uneasily
   - □ b. firmly
   - □ c. briefly

2. The idea had seemed so **reasonable**
   when it had first occurred to him.
   - □ a. unbelievable
   - □ b. impossible
   - □ c. sensible

3. . . . a **vacant** house with no one to
   tend it, four little dogs that needed
   a place to stay. . . .
   - □ a. busy
   - □ b. sturdy
   - □ c. empty

4. . . . she had formed a deep **attachment**
   for the group in the sewing closet.
   - □ a. dislike
   - □ b. affection
   - □ c. purpose

5. "Does your school have a bulletin
   board? You could pin up a sort of
   announcement—"
   - □ a. award
   - □ b. order
   - □ c. message

6. "I can't understand it," she said in
   bewilderment, as she joined the rest
   of the family in the dining room.
   - □ a. confusion
   - □ b. happiness
   - □ c. carelessness

7. "Perhaps she's gone to someone's
   house," Mr. Walker **suggested**.
   - □ a. cried
   - □ b. asked
   - □ c. mentioned

8. He had never been able to tell a lie
   successfully, even a little one.
   - □ a. clearly
   - □ b. well
   - □ c. badly

Birth of an Island

Millicent E. Selsam

Reading Time ▢ ▢ Maze

Comprehension ▢ ▢ Vocabulary

This passage was taken from *Birth of an Island* by Millicent E. Selsam. The book tells how islands form in the oceans of the world. If you would like to read more about this subject, ask for the book at either your school or neighborhood library.

Many thousands of years ago, far off in the middle of a big ocean, miles from the nearest land, a crack opened in an undersea volcano. With a rumble and a roar, an explosion of red hot lava and burning ashes burst forth. Huge black clouds swirled to the sky. The water boiled and white steam mixed with the fiery cloud.

The hot lava piled higher and higher and spread wider and wider. In this way, slowly, an island rose up in the sea.

The hot lava cooled and stiffened into shining black rock. Hot sun beat down on the rock. Cool rains fell. Now hot, now cold, the rock split and gradually broke to pieces. In the course of time, a fine crumbly soil covered the island. Where the rock met the sea, waves dashed against it, tore away pieces, and ground them to sand.

Nothing lived on the naked soil. Not as yet. But slowly, through the years, the island became covered with green plants. And slowly, animals began to move over its beaches and hills. How did they get there?

This story will be about a tropical island surrounded by warm seas. But the way the plants and animals come to this little bit of earth in the sea is the story of how plants and animals have spread from one island to another all over the world.

Around the island the wind roared, the ocean crashed, and the birds flapped their wings. The wind, the sea, and the birds were at work bringing life to the new island.

From the land nearest the new island, the wind picked up seeds light as dust, seeds with delicate airy parachutes or silky hairs that kept them drifting through the air. And from land near and far the wind brought little spiders and other insects so light they could sail on the air currents. But the wind was also loaded with invisible clouds of living things too tiny to see. Millions of the world's smallest plants—the bacteria—floated in the air. Some of these fell on the island and multiplied. Countless dustlike cells called spores were carried by the wind. These too fell on the island and sprouted, like seeds. Some grew into algae—the simplest plants made up of single cells or thin sheets of cells. Others grew into molds. Some were the spores of ferns.

Although the wind brought so many living things to the island, only the plants could grow there at first. Only they, in sunlight, could manufacture food from the minerals of the soil, water, and the carbon dioxide of the air. While many animals landed on the island, they could find no food. A spider spun its web in vain, because there were no insects it could catch in its silky threads. Insects couldn't stay until there were plants for them to eat. So the plants had to be the pioneer life on this island.

COMPREHENSION

Read the following questions and statements. For each one, put an _x_ in the box before the option that contains the most complete or accurate answer. Check your answers using the Answer Key on page 206.

1. A new island is
   □ a. made from its own rock.
   □ b. brought by the wind.
   □ c. carried in by birds.

2. Most of the new life is brought to the island by
   □ a. ocean currents.
   □ b. fish and animals.
   □ c. wind and birds.

3. According to the story, plants grow from seeds and
   □ a. soil.
   □ b. spores.
   □ c. eggs.

4. What first grew on the island?
   □ a. plants
   □ b. animals
   □ c. people

5. Plants are the only thing that
   □ a. can live off the soil, water, and air.
   □ b. can get to the island.
   □ c. need salt water to stay alive.

6. If an animal could find no food on the island it would
   □ a. make food.
   □ b. die.
   □ c. hibernate.

7. Which sentence best describes the growth of life on a new island?
   □ a. Anything can come to a new island and find food right away.
   □ b. Everything that is going to live on the island is there when the island is formed.
   □ c. Life forms on a new island in stages.

8. The author of this selection is showing the reader how
   □ a. volcanoes have destroyed cities.
   □ b. different soil types affect plant growth.
   □ c. life grows and spreads throughout the world.

The following passage, taken from the selection you have just read, has words omitted from it. Fill in each blank using a word from the set of five words in the column to the right of the passage. Check your answers using the Answer Key on page 206.

Many thousands of years ago, far off in the middle of a big ocean, miles from the nearest land, a crack opened in an undersea _____ .
1
With a rumble and a roar, an _____ of red hot
2
lava and burning ashes burst forth. Huge black _____ swirled to
3
the sky. The water boiled and white steam mixed with the fiery cloud.

The hot lava piled higher and higher and _____ wider and
4
wider. In this way, slowly, an island rose up in the sea.

The hot _____
5
cooled and stiffened into shining black _____ . Hot
6
sun beat down on the rock. Cool rains fell. Now hot, now cold, the rock split and gradually broke to _____ . In the course
7
of time, a fine crumbly soil covered the _____ . Where the
8
rock met the sea, waves dashed against it, tore away pieces, and ground them to sand.

1. a. volcano   b. area   c. bed
    d. rock   e. land

2. a. increase b. explosion c. amount
    d. exhaustion   e. expulsion

3. a. steam   b. water   c. smoke
    d. clouds   e. ash

4. a. flew   b. piled   c. spread
    d. flowed   e. cracked

5. a. cloud   b. rock   c. lava
    d. ash   e. steam

6. a. pieces   b. soil   c. sea
    d. rock   e. sand

7. a. bits   b. stones   c. soil
    d. sand   e. pieces

8. a. island   b. rock   c. lava
    d. sea   e. land

VOCABULARY

Look at the word in boldface in each exercise that follows and read carefully the sentence with it. Put an *x* in the box before the best meaning or synonym for the word as it is used in the sentence. Check your answers using the Answer Key on page 206.

1. Huge black clouds **swirled** to the sky.
   - ☐ a. twisted up
   - ☐ b. fell down
   - ☐ c. jumped over

2. The hot **lava** cooled and stiffened into shining black rock.
   - ☐ a. melted rock
   - ☐ b. clouds of steam
   - ☐ c. powdery ashes

3. Where the rock met the sea, waves **dashed** against it, tore away pieces, and ground them to sand.
   - ☐ a. hit roughly
   - ☐ b. ran quickly
   - ☐ c. rolled peacefully

4. But the way the plants and animals come to this little bit of earth in the sea is the story of how plants and animals have **spread** from one island to another all over the world.
   - ☐ a. scattered around
   - ☐ b. covered with a thin layer
   - ☐ c. vanished forever

5. . . . the wind picked up seeds light as dust, seeds with **delicate** airy parachutes or silky hairs that kept them drifting through the air.
   - ☐ a. prickly
   - ☐ b. heavy and thick
   - ☐ c. thin and easily torn

6. . . . the wind brought little spiders and other insects so light they could sail on the air **currents**.
   - ☐ a. heights
   - ☐ b. flows
   - ☐ c. pockets

7. . . . spores were carried by the wind. These too fell on the island and **sprouted**, like seeds.
   - ☐ a. bounced
   - ☐ b. blew away
   - ☐ c. began to grow

8. A spider spun its web in **vain**, because there were no insects it could catch in its silky threads.
   - ☐ a. with pride
   - ☐ b. without success
   - ☐ c. with help

Answer Key

Answer Key

Set 1

1•1 Tuck Everlasting

COMPREHENSION		MAZE		VOCABULARY	
1. b	5. c	1. e	5. c	1. b	5. c
2. a	6. b	2. e	6. c	2. c	6. a
3. b	7. a	3. b	7. e	3. a	7. c
4. c	8. c	4. d	8. c	4. a	8. b

1•2 The Adventures of the Black Cowboys

COMPREHENSION		MAZE		VOCABULARY	
1. a	5. b	1. d	5. c	1. a	5. c
2. a	6. c	2. e	6. a	2. a	6. a
3. c	7. c	3. a	7. b	3. b	7. a
4. b	8. b	4. b	8. d	4. b	8. b

1•3 A Taste of Blackberries

COMPREHENSION		MAZE		VOCABULARY	
1. a	5. b	1. d	5. c	1. a	5. b
2. b	6. a	2. a	6. d	2. c	6. c
3. c	7. c	3. b	7. b	3. c	7. c
4. b	8. b	4. e	8. b	4. a	8. b

1•4 How to Lasso a Shark

COMPREHENSION		MAZE		VOCABULARY	
1. a	5. b	1. d	5. d	1. a	5. b
2. b	6. b	2. c	6. c	2. c	6. c
3. b	7. c	3. a	7. c	3. a	7. b
4. a	8. b	4. e	8. a	4. b	8. c

1•5 J. T.

COMPREHENSION		MAZE		VOCABULARY	
1. c	5. c	1. b	5. d	1. b	5. a
2. b	6. b	2. e	6. d	2. b	6. a
3. c	7. a	3. a	7. a	3. a	7. b
4. c	8. c	4. c	8. d	4. a	8. c

Set 2

2•1 Mystery Monsters of Loch Ness

COMPREHENSION		MAZE		VOCABULARY	
1. c	5. c	1. b	5. a	1. b	5. a
2. b	6. b	2. d	6. c	2. c	6. c
3. b	7. c	3. a	7. c	3. c	7. b
4. a	8. a	4. e	8. a	4. b	8. a

2•2 The Great Brain at the Academy

COMPREHENSION		MAZE		VOCABULARY	
1. a	5. c	1. a	5. b	1. b	5. b
2. b	6. a	2. d	6. d	2. b	6. c
3. a	7. b	3. c	7. d	3. c	7. b
4. c	8. b	4. c	8. b	4. a	8. c

2•3 Wilt Chamberlain

COMPREHENSION		MAZE		VOCABULARY	
1. a	5. b	1. e	5. d	1. a	5. a
2. b	6. a	2. c	6. b	2. c	6. b
3. c	7. c	3. a	7. c	3. a	7. b
4. a	8. a	4. c	8. a	4. a	8. b

2•4 From the Mixed-Up Files of Mrs. Basil E. Frankweiler

COMPREHENSION		MAZE		VOCABULARY	
1. b	5. c	1. d	5. e	1. a	5. a
2. c	6. b	2. a	6. a	2. c	6. c
3. b	7. a	3. c	7. c	3. b	7. a
4. b	8. b	4. d	8. d	4. b	8. c

2•5 The World of Robots

COMPREHENSION		MAZE		VOCABULARY	
1. c	5. b	1. c	5. d	1. c	5. c
2. a	6. a	2. e	6. c	2. c	6. b
3. c	7. a	3. a	7. a	3. b	7. a
4. b	8. c	4. b	8. c	4. b	8. b

Set 3

3•1 Mom, You're Fired!

COMPREHENSION		MAZE		VOCABULARY	
1. c	5. c	1. c	5. d	1. a	5. b
2. b	6. a	2. a	6. b	2. b	6. c
3. c	7. c	3. a	7. b	3. a	7. a
4. c	8. a	4. e	8. d	4. a	8. a

3•2 We Live in Mexico

COMPREHENSION		MAZE		VOCABULARY	
1. b	5. a	1. c	5. d	1. a	5. a
2. a	6. c	2. a	6. a	2. b	6. c
3. c	7. c	3. c	7. c	3. b	7. c
4. a	8. a	4. d	8. e	4. a	8. a

3•3 Pippi Longstocking

COMPREHENSION		MAZE		VOCABULARY	
1. a	5. a	1. d	5. a	1. b	5. b
2. c	6. b	2. a	6. d	2. a	6. c
3. b	7. a	3. c	7. a	3. b	7. a
4. c	8. c	4. e	8. e	4. a	8. c

3•4 James and the Giant Peach

COMPREHENSION		MAZE		VOCABULARY	
1. b	5. c	1. c	5. a	1. b	5. c
2. b	6. b	2. e	6. d	2. a	6. a
3. c	7. b	3. d	7. b	3. a	7. b
4. a	8. a	4. d	8. b	4. a	8. a

3•5 Little House in the Big Woods

COMPREHENSION		MAZE		VOCABULARY	
1. b	5. a	1. b	5. a	1. b	5. b
2. a	6. c	2. e	6. c	2. a	6. c
3. a	7. b	3. a	7. e	3. a	7. a
4. b	8. b	4. b	8. d	4. c	8. a

Set 4

4•1 Racing on the Wind

COMPREHENSION		MAZE		VOCABULARY	
1. b	5. b	1. e	5. a	1. a	5. b
2. a	6. c	2. b	6. d	2. a	6. b
3. b	7. b	3. d	7. a	3. c	7. c
4. b	8. c	4. e	8. a	4. b	8. a

4•2 Henry Reed's Journey

COMPREHENSION		MAZE		VOCABULARY	
1. b	5. a	1. c	5. b	1. c	5. c
2. b	6. b	2. b	6. a	2. a	6. c
3. a	7. a	3. c	7. b	3. b	7. a
4. c	8. b	4. b	8. d	4. b	8. b

4•3 Behind the Scenes of a Broadway Musical

COMPREHENSION		MAZE		VOCABULARY	
1. c	5. b	1. e	5. a	1. b	5. c
2. c	6. c	2. c	6. b	2. a	6. b
3. a	7. b	3. b	7. e	3. c	7. a
4. a	8. b	4. b	8. c	4. a	8. b

4•4 The Good-Guy Cake

COMPREHENSION		MAZE		VOCABULARY	
1. c	5. a	1. d	5. d	1. b	5. a
2. a	6. b	2. c	6. b	2. c	6. a
3. b	7. c	3. a	7. a	3. a	7. b
4. c	8. a	4. d	8. c	4. b	8. a

4•5 Gravity

COMPREHENSION		MAZE		VOCABULARY	
1. b	5. c	1. b	5. e	1. a	5. a
2. c	6. b	2. d	6. c	2. c	6. b
3. a	7. a	3. e	7. c	3. b	7. c
4. a	8. a	4. c	8. a	4. c	8. a

Set 5

5•1 The Enormous Egg

COMPREHENSION		MAZE		VOCABULARY	
1. b	5. c	1. d	5. a	1. b	5. c
2. a	6. c	2. c	6. c	2. b	6. c
3. a	7. a	3. c	7. a	3. c	7. a
4. c	8. b	4. e	8. a	4. b	8. a

5•2 A Good Friend Is . . .

COMPREHENSION		MAZE		VOCABULARY	
1. c	5. b	1. c	5. e	1. b	5. c
2. b	6. a	2. c	6. b	2. a	6. a
3. b	7. c	3. a	7. c	3. a	7. b
4. b	8. a	4. a	8. d	4. c	8. c

5•3 The Cartoonist

COMPREHENSION		MAZE		VOCABULARY	
1. a	5. a	1. d	5. d	1. b	5. a
2. b	6. a	2. c	6. c	2. c	6. c
3. c	7. c	3. a	7. a	3. b	7. b
4. c	8. b	4. a	8. b	4. c	8. c

5•4 Set Your Sails For Fun!

COMPREHENSION		MAZE		VOCABULARY	
1. b	5. c	1. b	5. c	1. c	5. c
2. a	6. a	2. b	6. a	2. b	6. a
3. c	7. b	3. b	7. c	3. a	7. c
4. c	8. b	4. c	8. d	4. a	8. b

5•5 A Bear Called Paddington

COMPREHENSION		MAZE		VOCABULARY	
1. b	5. c	1. d	5. d	1. c	5. a
2. b	6. a	2. b	6. c	2. a	6. b
3. a	7. a	3. d	7. a	3. c	7. a
4. c	8. c	4. c	8. b	4. b	8. b

Set 6

6•1 To See Half the World

COMPREHENSION		MAZE		VOCABULARY	
1. a	5. c	1. d	5. a	1. a	5. b
2. a	6. c	2. b	6. b	2. c	6. b
3. b	7. b	3. a	7. e	3. b	7. b
4. a	8. a	4. b	8. a	4. a	8. c

6•2 Charlie and the Chocolate Factory

COMPREHENSION		MAZE		VOCABULARY	
1. b	5. c	1. e	5. a	1. a	5. b
2. c	6. b	2. c	6. c	2. a	6. b
3. a	7. b	3. b	7. b	3. c	7. c
4. c	8. a	4. e	8. c	4. c	8. a

6•3 They Study the Ocean

COMPREHENSION		MAZE		VOCABULARY	
1. b	5. b	1. a	5. e	1. b	5. a
2. c	6. c	2. c	6. a	2. c	6. b
3. b	7. a	3. c	7. d	3. b	7. c
4. a	8. a	4. d	8. a	4. b	8. a

6•4 Hotel for Dogs

COMPREHENSION		MAZE		VOCABULARY	
1. b	5. c	1. c	5. d	1. b	5. c
2. c	6. b	2. b	6. a	2. c	6. a
3. c	7. c	3. e	7. c	3. c	7. c
4. b	8. a	4. b	8. e	4. b	8. b

6•5 Birth of an Island

COMPREHENSION		MAZE		VOCABULARY	
1. a	5. a	1. a	5. c	1. a	5. c
2. c	6. b	2. b	6. d	2. a	6. b
3. b	7. c	3. d	7. e	3. a	7. c
4. a	8. c	4. c	8. a	4. a	8. b

Words per Minute

Words per Minute

Reading Time	Words per Minute	Reading Time	Words per Minute
1:00	500	4:40	107
1:10	431	4:50	104
1:20	376	**5:00**	100
1:30	333	5:10	97
1:40	301	5:20	94
1:50	273	5:30	91
2:00	250	5:40	88
2:10	231	5:50	86
2:20	215	**6:00**	83
2:30	200	6:10	81
2:40	188	6:20	79
2:50	177	6:30	77
3:00	167	6:40	75
3:10	158	6:50	73
3:20	150	**7:00**	71
3:30	143	7:10	70
3:40	137	7:20	68
3:50	131	7:30	67
4:00	125	7:40	65
4:10	120	7:50	64
4:20	115	**8:00**	63
4:30	111		

Progress Graphs

Reading Speed

Directions. Use the graph below to show your reading speed improvement.

First, along the top of the graph, find the number of the story you just read. Notice the line going down to the bottom of the graph under that number. Second, along the left side of the graph, find your reading time. Notice the line going across the graph from your reading time to your number of words per minute. Put an *x* where the two lines cross.

As you enter *x*'s for other stories, connect them with a line. This will help you see right away if your reading speed is going up as it should be. If the line connecting the *x*'s is not going up, see your teacher for advice.

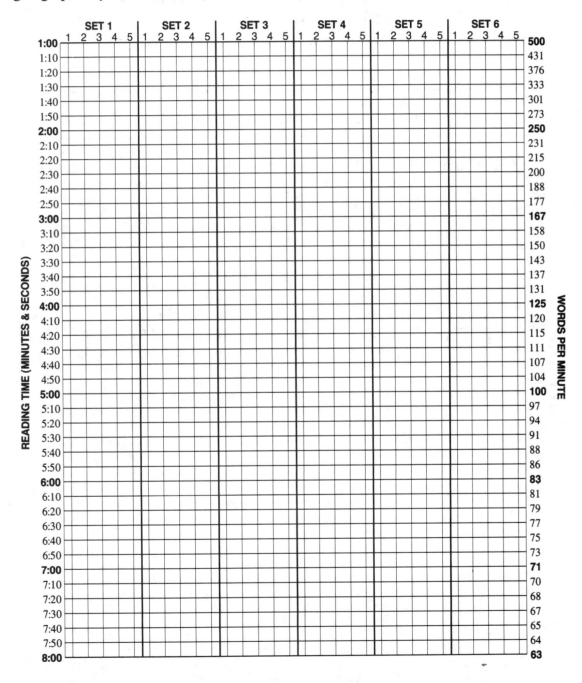

Comprehension

Directions. Use the graph below to show your comprehension scores.

First, along the top of the graph, find the number of the story you have just read. Notice the line going down to the bottom of the graph under that number. Second, along the left side of the graph, find the number which shows how many questions you got right. Notice the line going across the graph from your number correct to your percent score. Put an *x* where the two lines cross.

As you plot more comprehension scores, connect the *x*'s with a line. The line will help you see right away if your scores are going up or down. If your comprehension scores are below 75%, or if they are going down, see your teacher. Try to keep your scores at 75% or above while you keep building your reading speed.

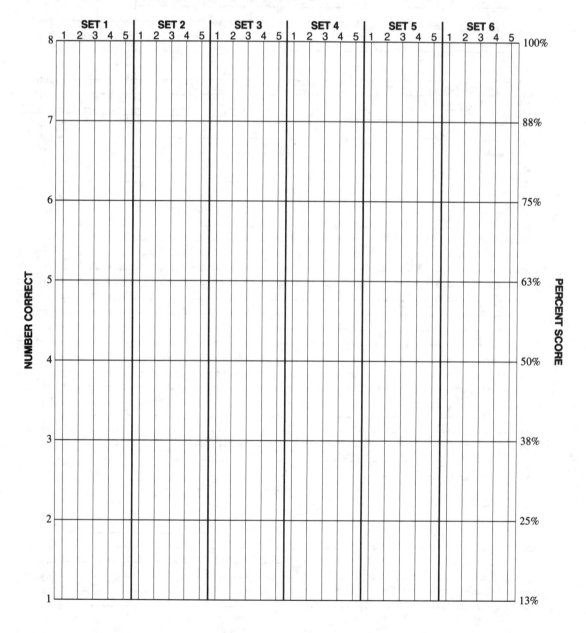

Maze

Directions. Use the graph below to show your scores on the maze tests.

First, along the top of the graph, find the number of the story you have just read. Notice the line going down to the bottom of the graph under that number. Second, along the left side of the graph, find the number which shows how many questions you got right. Notice the line going across the graph from that number to your percent score. Put an *x* where the two lines cross.

As you plot your scores on the rest of the maze tests, connect the *x*'s with a line. The line will help you see right away if your scores are going up or down. If your scores are below 50%, or if they are going down, see your teacher. Try to keep your scores at 50% or above as you continue to build your reading speed.

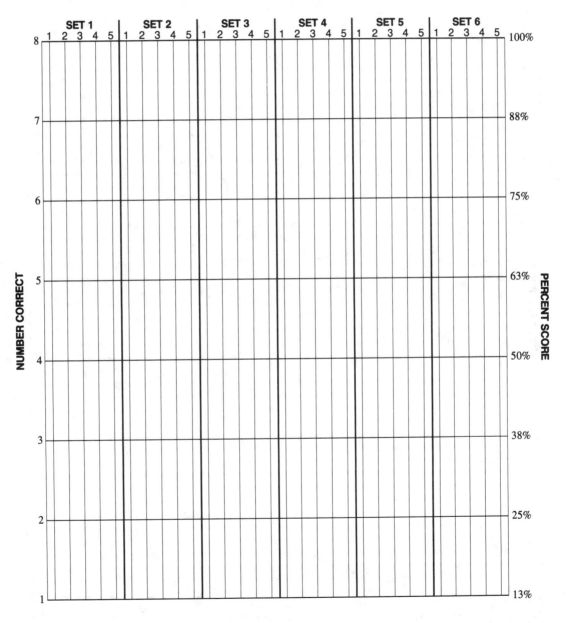

Vocabulary

Directions. Use the graph below to show your vocabulary scores.

First, along the top of the graph, find the number of the story you have just read. Notice the line going down to the bottom of the graph under that number. Second, along the left side of the graph, find the number which shows how many vocabulary questions you got right. Notice the line going across the graph from that number to your percent score. Put an *x* where the two lines cross.

As you plot more vocabulary scores, connect the *x*'s with a line. The line will help you see right away if your scores are going up or down. If your vocabulary scores are not going up, see your teacher for advice. Vocabulary scores of 75% are good, but try to earn scores of 88% and 100% when you can.

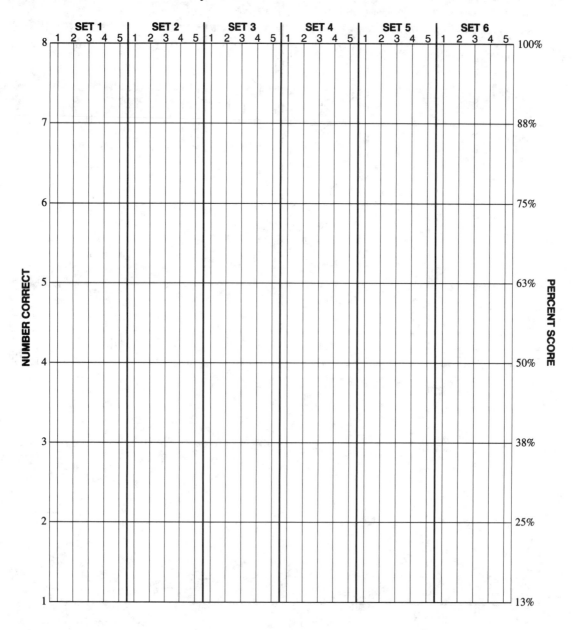

Picture Credits

1-1 Tuck Everlasting: Illustration from TUCK EVERLASTING by Natalie Babbitt. Copyright © 1975 by Natalie Babbitt. Reprinted by permission of Farrar, Straus and Giroux, Inc.

1-2 The Adventures of the Black Cowboys: "Pull at the Canteen" by Frederic Remington

1-3 A Taste of Blackberries: Illustration by Charles Robinson from A TASTE OF BLACKBERRIES by Doris Buchanan Smith. Reprinted by permission of Scholastic, Inc.

1-4 How to Lasso a Shark: Brian Parker/TOM STACK & ASSOCIATES

1-5 J. T.: Photo by Gordon Parks Jr. from J. T. by Jane Wagner, © 1969

2-1 Mystery Monsters of Loch Ness: AP/WIDE WORLD PHOTOS

2-2 The Great Brain at the Academy: Illustration by Mercer Mayer from THE GREAT BRAIN AT THE ACADEMY by John D. Fitzgerald. Reprinted by permission of E. P. Dutton.

2-3 Wilt Chamberlain: AP/WIDE WORLD PHOTOS

2-4 From the Mixed-Up Files of Mrs. Basil E. Frankweiler: Photo from FROM THE MIXED-UP FILES OF MRS. BASIL E. FRANKWEILER by E. L. Konigsburg, copyright © 1967

2-5 The World of Robots: Betts Anderson/ UNICORN STOCK PHOTOS

3-1 Mom, You're Fired! Illustration by Rich Bishop

3-2 We Live in Mexico: Dan Peha

3-3 Pippi Longstocking: Illustration by Lenny Long

3-4 James and the Giant Peach: Illustration by Nancy Eckholm Burkert, from *James and the Giant Peach* by Roald Dahl, copyright 1961, Random House, Inc.

3-5 Little House in the Big Woods: Illustration by Lenny Long

4-1 Racing on the Wind: Earl L. Kubis/ Root Resources

4-2 Henry Reed's Journey: Illustration by Robert McCloskey from HENRY REED'S JOURNEY by Keith Robertson. Copyright © 1963 by Robert McCloskey. All rights reserved. Reprinted by permission of Viking Penguin, Inc.

4-3 Behind the Scenes of a Broadway Musical: Photo from BEHIND THE SCENES OF A BROADWAY MUSICAL by Bill Powers. Reprinted by permission of Crown Publishers, Inc.

4-4 The Good-Guy Cake: © Morrow Junior Books (A Division of William Morrow and Company, Inc.)

4-5 Gravity: Illustration by Rich Bishop

5-1 The Enormous Egg: Illustration by Lenny Long

5-2 A Good Friend Is . . .: Photo by H. Finch

5-3 The Cartoonist: Jacket illustration by Richard Cuffari from THE CARTOONIST by Betsy Byars. All rights reserved. Reprinted by permission of Viking Penguin Inc.

5-4 Set Your Sails For Fun! Photo by Michael Morrison

5-5 A Bear Called Paddington: Illustration by Lenny Long

6-1 To See Half the World: Jack Stein Grove/ Photo Edit

6-2 Charlie and the Chocolate Factory: Illustration by Lenny Long

6-3 They Study the Ocean: © 1981/Peter Wiebe, Woods Hole Oceanographic Institution

6-4 Hotel for Dogs: Illustration by Leonard Shortall

1-2 Birth of an Island: © Joe Viesti